North Shields
Public Houses
Inns & Taverns
Part One

by Charlie Steel

The Angel Hotel, later the Olde Hundred, Albion Street / Church Way, c.1897.

Previous page: The Prince of Wales, Liddell Street with the famous Wooden Doll – giving the pub the nickname 'The Old Wooden Doll'.

Summerhill Books

Summerhill Books publishes local history books on Northumberland, Durham and Tyneside. To receive a catalogue of our titles send a stamped addressed envelope to:

Andrew Clark, Summerhill Books, PO Box 1210, Newcastle-upon-Tyne NE99 4AH

or email: summerhillbooks@yahoo.co.uk

or visit our website to view our full range of books: **www.summerhillbooks.co.uk**

Copyright Charlie Steel 2013

First published in 2013 by

Summerhill Books
PO Box 1210, Newcastle-upon-Tyne NE99 4AH

www.summerhillbooks.co.uk

email: summerhillbooks@yahoo.co.uk

ISBN: 978-1-906721-64-0

CONTENTS

The Albion Hotel, Norfolk Street / Saville Street. c.1894.

INTRODUCTION

This book is a completely new and fully updated version of my previous book 'Inns and Taverns of North Shields' originally published by Tempus in 2007. Along with additional photographs, the individual listings in this version are more comprehensive, many of which also interpret the origins and names of the particular establishments.

This book is confined solely to the main part of North Shields; however Volume Two will include those premises on the outskirts of the town such as Percy Main, Chirton, and Preston etc. along with neighbouring Tynemouth, Cullercoats, Whitley Bay, Monkseaton and Earsdon.

I have spent thousands of hours of research, trawling through old directories and licensing records to compile what I consider to be a fairly comprehensive list or gazetteer of all the inns, taverns, ale houses, hotels and beer sellers recorded in North Shields from 1822 to the present day. Of course, old records cannot be relied on to be 100% accurate and I therefore apologise to the reader for any errors or omissions which may become apparent – there are bound to be a few, particularly in relation to some of the dates which should be referred to only as a basic or generalised guide.

Research of this nature is quite complex, and involves seeking out many different sources to procure the required information, however drawbacks become apparent whenever a conflict of information is encountered. For example, it is common to find many variations in the spelling of words, names and places etc. and likewise dates can also conflict unless original copies of the relevant documentation are available to make them indisputable. Even old reference books or documents can be confusing and occasionally misleading, depending on how they are studied. Sometimes it requires logical interpretation and perhaps some calculated judgement to process and simplify that information to make it easily understood.

With that in mind, I have researched the information in this publication to the best of my ability, and attempted to ensure its accuracy as far as possible, however I am well aware that there will always be some details which are open to debate, especially those which may not be fully or correctly documented. If any obvious inaccuracies are found, it would be advantageous to advise me along with a provable reference source rather than being critical of the content, and this way with your help, they can be corrected for the benefit of any future editions.

The oldest directory I have been able to use during my research is dated 1822, and therefore this has been used as a general starting point for a number of the older premises listed in this book, however, many of them will have been built, constructed, converted or indeed established long before that date.

In using this book, it will be noted that some addresses shown for the same premises may differ, and this is attributable to various factors:

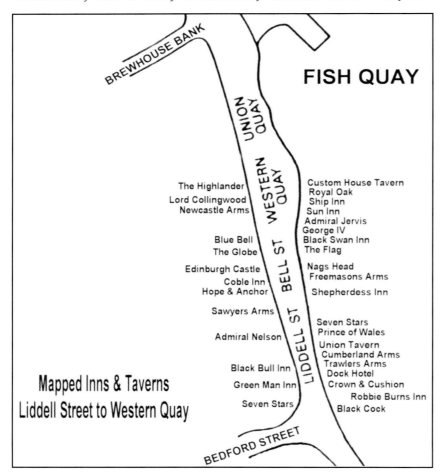

Mapped Inns & Taverns
Liddell Street to Western Quay

BREWHOUSE BANK

FISH QUAY

UNION QUAY

WESTERN QUAY

BELL ST

LIDDELL ST

The Highlander
Lord Collingwood
Newcastle Arms

Blue Bell
The Globe

Edinburgh Castle
Coble Inn
Hope & Anchor

Sawyers Arms

Admiral Nelson

Black Bull Inn

Green Man Inn

Seven Stars

Custom House Tavern
Royal Oak
Ship Inn
Sun Inn
Admiral Jervis
George IV
Black Swan Inn
The Flag

Nags Head
Freemasons Arms

Shepherdess Inn

Seven Stars
Prince of Wales
Union Tavern
Cumberland Arms
Trawlers Arms
Dock Hotel
Crown & Cushion
Robbie Burns Inn
Black Cock

BEDFORD STREET

1) Over the years, Tynemouth council introduced a system whereby some streets in the borough were changed, renamed or renumbered, which effectively meant that many of the premises on that street were subjected to an unavoidable change of address. (Perhaps a good example of this is the Alnwick Castle pub, which is recorded at Nos. 26 & 28 Saville Street and also at Nos. 22 & 112 Church Way, North Shields.)

2) It was fairly common for a pub to be built on the corner of two streets and therefore that pub may be listed in directories as appearing on either one or even both of those streets. This in turn could become confusing where the street may have also been subject to renumbering, hence any apparent discrepancies.

3) Sometimes, road or street names would change, or they may have been better known by a local name. For example: Albion Street became Albion Road, and Lower Pearson Street became Charlotte Street. Some streets were sub-named, such as Cobourg Terrace which forms part of Tynemouth Road.

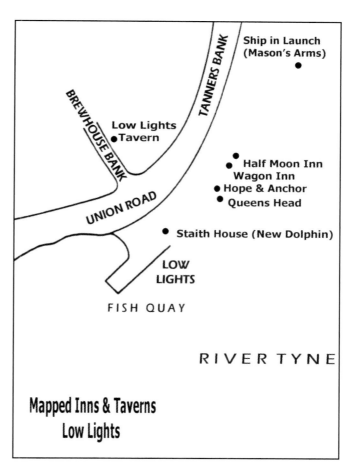

Mapped Inns & Taverns
Low Lights

4) Occasionally, there may be anomalies where there was no defined boundary as to where a continuous road began or ended, such as in the Low Town where Clive Street continued into Liddell Street, which in turn merged with Bell Street, only to become Union Street or Union Quay within a short distance.

5) Many inns and taverns themselves have also undergone several name changes over a period of time. They may also have been known by local names, variations of a name or even nicknames. Combined with apparent address changes, this has made it difficult to establish and confirm the identity of many of the older individual pubs with any degree of certainty, and therefore there may be some repetition or omissions.

6) Also, some of the older directories used in the compilation of this book were not always 100% accurate in their content, and therefore allowances need to be taken into consideration for possible errors.

As a relatively small town in the 1800s, North Shields has probably had the highest number of inns, taverns, ale houses and beer sellers to be found anywhere in the country. The Low Town in particular had an extremely high concentration of pubs, with some Inns actually adjoining each other, and others just being a matter of feet away from the next. Between 1822 to the present day, approximately 440 inns, taverns and ale houses have been recorded in North Shields covering a time span of around 200 years. These numbers do not include the small independent ale, porter, wine & spirit merchants, and brewers which themselves numbered in excess of 225.

The largest volume of Public Houses was approximately 180 in North Shields High Town, 158 in the Low Town, and 83 in the west end and Bull Ring area of the town. The Chirton and Percy Main areas comprised around 17 Public Houses, and Preston Township had 14 known inns and taverns. (It should however be remembered that not all of these premises existed at any one time.)

I hope this book proves to be an interesting source of reference, and that you enjoy reading it.

Charlie Steel
May 2013

NORTH SHIELDS OVERVIEW

In 1225, the Prior of Tynemouth built 27 huts or 'Shielings' in which to house his workers at the Pow Burn, situated to the east of the present Fish Quay. This small settlement rapidly grew to a thriving township of over 100 dwellings, and by the end of the 13th century, included a quay landing, wharves, a brewery, mills & bake houses, and so the development of North Shields began.

The origin of the name North Shields is somewhat uncertain, but it is probable that it was derived from these 'Shielings', which were often referred to as 'Sheels' on the north side of the river.

It has often been said that the best way to learn history is to study castles and churches; however it cannot be denied that the best way to learn about the history of North Shields, is to study the Pubs!

In 1853, it was estimated that there were 217 public houses, taverns and ale houses in the Borough of Tynemouth, which included North Shields, Tynemouth and Cullercoats.

North Shields itself consists of two parts; The High Town and the Low Town. The High Town was basically the Town Centre and the area above the river that was built on the 'High Ground'.

The Low Town comprised all the buildings, streets, quays and stairs below the High Town, and ran down the steep banks to the riverside, from near the site of the present Tanners Bank to the New Quay, with many of the quays here actually deriving their names from people or local inns.

The narrow winding street running parallel with the river, and running from east to west made up Union Road, Union Quay, Western Quay, Bell Street, Liddell Street, Clive Street and Duke Street, which in some places was so tight that it was only possible for one horse and cart to pass through at a time.

Houses, Shops and Inns were crowded against each other along the streets, and access to the river was via narrow alleyways and quays. Dozens of stairs lined the steep banks to connect the Low Town with the High Town, and provide access to the hundreds of crowded tenement buildings which were constructed along the length of the bank sides. These buildings were nothing more than slums, infested with rats and vermin, and even as far back as the mid 1800s they were recorded as being the refuge of scum and the lowest dregs of society.

In the 1700s and 1800s, the Low Town was rife with petty thieves and prostitutes and could be a dangerous and formidable place. The area was generally out of bounds for any self-respecting citizen to venture, especially during the hours of darkness as muggings were widespread, crime was commonplace, and Press Gangs were known to scour the waterfront to board suitable men for conscription and impressment.

An illustration of North Shields Quayside from 1898.

Clive Street, c.1950.

There was a high concentration of public houses in the Low Town of North Shields, where at one time, there were 16 pubs on Clive Street alone.

Many of the taverns and ale houses in this area were dirty, seedy drinking dens of vice and intemperance, dimly lit with tallow candles, where drunkenness was commonplace and many unlawful and immoral schemes were plotted.

Most of these dens of iniquity have long since disappeared, and by 2013, the only old establishments left in the Low Town were; The New Dolphin, The Low Lights, The Prince of Wales and the Golden Fleece (since renamed as The Porthole).

Despite its reputation, North Shields was recognised as a thriving and bustling fishing port, but during the 20th century, quayside activities declined, and as a result, many of the old buildings and concentrated masses of tenement houses and slums that once filled the bank sides were demolished; leaving only a few plaques, which serve as a reminder to indicate the sites of many of the old quays and stairs.

Although the streets of the Low Town still exist to this day, it can be difficult to imagine how the area looked during the 1800s, and while those dark days of North Shields Low Town are now long gone, most of the area is virtually unrecognisable today as a schedule of continual redevelopment progresses.

Much of the old Low Town is now overlooked by modern houses, flats and apartments, and has become a fashionable area in which to live as well as being a popular venue with families who visit the restaurants, shops and attractions which now line the riverside and Fish Quay areas.

Since these early beginnings, North Shields has grown into the town it is today leaving a wealth of history in its wake.

Poverty in the old Low Town – inside one home in Clive Street, c.1930.

THE ENGLISH PUB

When the first English road was built, the first English 'pub' was born. The date of that event – no man knows, but from that day to this, the ale house, inn and tavern have been an essential part of English life as well as a delightful feature of the English scene. The term 'public house' was first used during the 17th century and with at least one in almost every village, the term 'pub' or 'public house' is a general term or definition loosely used to describe any ale house, inn or tavern.

In the United Kingdom, a visitor needing directions is usually guided to his destination not by churches or street names, but by pub names. In many places, a pub can be the focal point of the community, playing a similar role to the local church in this respect. The old coaching inns also played an important role in days gone by, and can usually be identified by a large arched entrance leading to a courtyard, where stabling for horses, and accommodation facilities were provided to the traveller.

"This tavern is dedicated to those excellent gentlemen who make drinking a pleasure, who reach contentment before capacity, and who, whatever they drink, can take it, hold it, and still remain gentlemen."

In one way or another, and throughout history, the English Pub has been placed at the heart of our social culture, as they tend to be a canvas against which the drama of our daily lives is played out. Relationships are made and broken, sorrows drowned, and successes toasted. Whatever the occasion or reason, it is because we are a nation that likes to drink.

At the time of the Norman Conquest, William of Malmesbury wrote: *"Drinking in particular is a universal practice, in which occupation entire nights as well as days are passed away. The English were accustomed to eat till they became surfeited, and drank until they were sick."*

The English defeat at the hands of the Norman invader was put down to drink, the natives fighting more with rashness and precipitate fury than with military skill. The writer and presenter Jeremy Paxman once stated: *"That the English, far from being ashamed of their behaviour, see fighting and drunkenness as part of their birthright. It is the way they proclaim their identity."*

In 1831, an observer wrote; *"Everybody is drunk. Those who are not singing are sprawling."*

The historic role of the English drinking establishment is however, seen as a place of entertainment, accommodation and for the transaction of commerce.

In 1606, King James I passed two pieces of legislation, for the licensing of ale houses and the suppression of drunkenness. The title of the latter proclaimed its noble purpose: 'An Act for Repressing the Odious and Loathsome Sin of Drunkenness'. The legislation conspicuously failed, because further legislation was introduced in 1609: 'An Act for the Reformation of Ale House Keepers'. The monarch continued his programme of reform, which led to the first recorded example of licensing hours: The Newmarket Proclamation of James I in 1618. This required all inns and ale houses to close at 9pm and also during divine service on Sundays. During the protectorate of Oliver Cromwell (1653-58), King James imposed closure throughout Sundays, but the restrictions seem to have lapsed thereafter. While justices took it upon themselves to impose closing times, no national hours or days of trade were set again until 1839.

By the end of the 17th century, there was very little control over the supply of liquor, with licences freely granted by the justices, and rarely withdrawn, causing an expansion in the number of licensed premises, and the consumption of beer to increase by 1722 to 36 gallons a year for every man, woman and child.

At the end of the 18th century, licensing curtailments were imposed by Pitt's government in the Royal Proclamation Against Vice of 1757, passed against growing concerns that many licensed premises were becoming dens of iniquity, as well as places for the unemployed to plan their crimes or engage their gambling activities towards the savage and cruel sport of Cock-Fighting where many premises incorporated a 'Cock-Pit'. The proclamation declared the royal intention to punish 'All manner of vice, profaneness and immorality'. It forbade gambling on Sundays. It urged strict enforcement of laws against 'excessive drinking, blasphemy, profane swearing or cursing, lewdness, profanation of the Lord's Day, or other dissolute, immoral or disorderly practices.

In the early 19th century, there was a vast increase in alcohol consumption, particularly gin, and in 1830, The Duke of Wellington's Beer Act abolished duty on beer and ales in the hope of weaning some of the working classes off spirits, and an amazing 24,000 new beer shop licences were granted during the first year of the act, rising to 46,000 by 1836, and the number of public houses increased by 15% within 10 years of this legislation. The growth of public houses in England continued, and probably reached its peak during the latter half of the 1800s, however the past 100 years have seen a decline in numbers, although their popularity has never weakened.

Behind the bar of a traditional English pub.

The style of the English pub has changed dramatically over the years. At one time, a pub was simply a place to do little else but drink ale and engage in social merriment; however the traditional pub is at a serious risk of being lost as the commercial sector have seized on the opportunity to make vast profits by converting pubs into restaurants where a huge emphasis is put on high volume food sales rather than quality ales. If the trend is allowed to continue, then all that will be left in a few years is a fast food outlet that bears no resemblance whatsoever to the British pub.

Many other establishments have been converted to uncomfortable and unappealing theme bars with 'happy hours' and standing room only, or mini leisure centres where entire families can allegedly be 'entertained' with indoor and outdoor playgrounds, music, dancing, fruit machines, gaming machines, quizzes, and large screen televisions, whilst many of the old established and traditional bar games such as skittles, darts, dominoes, cribbage and even 'shove-ha'penny' have fallen into decline. Fizzy mass-produced pasteurised beers, lagers and 'alcopops' are now commonplace, with many noted names being consumed only because it is fashionable to drink certain brands from a bottle. This may have contributed to a change in the drinking culture, particularly amongst younger people which has led to concerns by the government over excessive alcohol consumption and the so-called 'binge-drinking' trend.

Fortunately, there are still a good number of traditional pubs left where the demand for real ales is high, and the average pub-goer drinks responsibly. For much of this, we need to be thankful to CAMRA (The Campaign for Real Ale), who have been instrumental in promoting and retaining this tradition over the past few years. In 2012 however, statistics indicate that up to five pubs are closing every day in the United Kingdom, and as the varied debates continue to rage on as to why this is happening, sadly there is little sign of any improvement.

The owner, tenant or manager (licensee) of a public house is known as the publican or landlord. In the UK a 'tied house' is a public house that is required to buy at least some of its beer from a particular brewery, unlike 'Free Houses', which are able to choose the beers they stock freely. The pub itself may be owned by the brewery in question, with the publican renting the pub from the brewery, this is termed a tenancy. Alternatively, the brewery may appoint a salaried manager to run the pub it owns, this form of tie can sometimes be termed a managed house. Finally, a publican may finance the purchase of a pub with soft

One of the most well know pubs in North Shields – The Prince of Wales, Liddell Street, c.1938.

loans from a brewer, and be required to buy his beer from them in return.

The traditional advantage of tied houses for breweries was the steadiness of demand they gave them – a tied house would not change its beers suddenly, so the brewer had a consistent market for their beer. However, this sometimes could victimise consumers, as when a regional brewer tied nearly every pub in an area, so it became very hard to drink anything but their beer. This was a form of monopoly opposed by CAMRA, especially when the brewer forced poor beer onto the market, due to the lack of competition from better breweries. Some or all drinks are then supplied by the brewery including spirits and soft drinks, quite often at an uncompetitive price relative to those paid by free houses. Since 1989 tied pubs in the UK have been legally permitted to stock at least one guest beer from another brewery to give greater choice to drinkers.

Further reading can be found in Paul Jennings book *The Local: A History of the English Pub* (Tempus, 2007)

At one time, beer and ale was supplied from various sized vessels of a set capacity, the names of which tend to be largely unheard of these days. They were colourfully referred to as follows:

Tun:	A large vessel containing 252 gallons.
Butt:	A smaller vessel containing 108 gallons.
Hogshead:	Equivalent to half a Butt, containing 54 gallons.
Barrel:	A size of cask or keg, containing 36 imperial gallons.
Kilderkin:	A half-barrel, containing 18 gallons.
Firkin:	A quarter barrel, containing 9 gallons.
Polypin:	Half a Firkin or 36 pints.
Quart:	2 pints or a quarter Gallon.

ORIGINS OF BEER

It is difficult to determine where ale was first brewed. Certainly it was known in the Tigris and Euphrates valleys before 4000 BC and it was known to the Babylonians in 2300 BC for one of their laws stated that a priestess going into an ale house to drink could be burned alive as a punishment. It is also said to have been introduced into Egypt by the god Osiris or his divine spouse Isis in 2017 BC. Beer was an important part of Egyptian diet

Neither is it known whether the inhabitants of Britain brewed ale before the Roman invasion but they were certainly doing so when the Romans left. The establishment of the Roman road network created the first inns, in which the weary traveller could obtain refreshment, and so the beginnings of the modern pub had been established. They became so commonplace that in 965 King Edgar decreed that there should be no more than one ale house per village. During the Roman occupation glass beakers and bowls were used for drinking but later, the art of glass making was lost, so earthenware pots and drinking horns were used.

Mazers or wooden drinking cups were also in use as were 'tumblers' – leather cups that had a rounded bottom and so tumbled over when they were put down. There were also peg-tankards which held about two quarts. Pegs inside the tankard divided the contents into eight parts so that each drinker, as the tankard was passed from hand to hand, had only his fair share. Hence comes the expression 'To have a peg'.

There were also, in the Middle Ages leather blackjacks. These were leather containers, of one-pint size, the insides of which had been treated with pitch. Mention must also be made of the bombard, a vessel made for the really mighty drinker, which could hold anything up to fifteen quarts! Of course, wealthy people drank from magnificently ornamented and jewelled cups and goblets of silver and gold.

In the year 1266 it was decided to regulate the price of ale by that of barley, and it is recorded that when barley was 2 shillings for 512 pounds in weight, ale was a farthing a quart. This was at a time when a labourer earned about nine-pence a day.

Hell's Kitchen – a notorious tavern in Newcastle, c.1820.

It is interesting to note that in those days ale was the general drink, being drunk at all times by young and old alike. Servants for instance, both male and female, usually had a piece of bread and a quart of ale for breakfast. In fact it is recorded, just after the Norman invasion, that the Canons of St. Paul's had a personal ration of 30 gallons of ale each week. This great consumption of ale may seem rather odd today, but it should be remembered that in those days there was nothing else to drink. Tea, coffee and cocoa were unknown and very little ordinary water was fit to drink unless one was fortunate enough to live near a natural spring or a small country stream. In addition it should be remembered that food was neither so plentiful nor varied as it is today, and as ale is a great source of nourishment as well as energy it was naturally a staple part of living.

It was not until the reign of Charles I that ale was taxed and his son Charles II further increased the tax in 1660 until it was 1s.3d a barrel on small beer.

It is not known when beer was brewed – you will have noticed that up till now the word ale has been exclusively used. The difference between the two is that ale was brewed only from malt, whereas beer was brewed from malt and hops. Be that as it may, the word beer was in common use by the year 1524 so it must have been some considerable time before that. New taxes were continually added to this indispensable beverage until they reached 4d a gallon before being repealed in 1830.

The first bottled beer was produced in the 17th century and it was an exceptionally strong beer, which was called stout. Porter was also first brewed about this time and was a cross between stout and beer.

It is interesting to note that until the middle of the 15th century the majority of brewing was done in the home. In 'The English Housewife' published early in the 17th century the following passage occurs: 'It is most requisite and fit that the Housewife be experienced and well practiced in the well making of malt, for as from it is made the drink by which the household is nourished and sustained'. As a result of this home brewing very little was done on a commercial scale and in 1585 there were only 26 brewers in London and its surroundings. When however, early in the 17th century tea arrived in England from the Far East and rapidly became a favourite drink among all classes, home brewing started to wane so that by 1685 there were 200 brewers in London and nearly 700 in the rest of the country. It is interesting to note that Trumans and Whitbread's were among the well-known early London brewers as were Bass and Worthington among the Burton brewers. As time passed the commercial brewers grew larger and many of them amalgamated and, with the advance of science, the art of brewing became exact instead of being, as it had for hundreds of years, merely a matter of rule of thumb.

For over a thousand years ale or beer was the staple drink of all the inhabitants of the British Isles but gradually this deep-rooted habit gave way before the onslaught of cheaper tea, coffee and cocoa, while the growth of many temperance societies banished it from numerous homes.

There are, naturally, many arguments for and against beer but most of those against it seem to stem from ignorance or prejudice and possibly the excesses of the few.

The plain and truthful fact is that beer is, as our forefathers well knew, a health-giving and

An advert for the brewers W.B. Reid & Co, Grey Street, Newcastle.

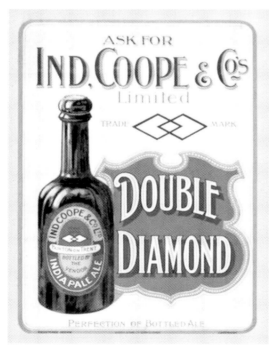

Ind. Coope & Co were one of a number of companies who had breweries in Burton-on-Trent.

invigorating beverage and one that even today, with its high taxation and comparatively low gravity, is still cheap. For instance, as a drink taken at any time, it has double the calorie value of the same quantity of tea or coffee. It also greatly enhances the value of any meal. Compare the average meal of today consisting of soup, beef, potatoes, cabbage, gravy and coffee with the old fashioned lunch of a pint of beer, three or four slices of buttered bread with cheese and a bit of lettuce, and two very startling facts emerge. The first is that an incontrovertible medical fact that the latter is a perfectly balanced meal in every way, which is more than can be said for the stodgy cooked meal. To put it in its simplest possible form, a pint of beer has the same energy giving value as four eggs or more than half a pound of meat!

Burton-on-Trent has been famous for ale and beer for many centuries. This is because, among other things, the water in this district has a high gypsum content, which renders it ideal for brewing. Burton ale was known in the time of Richard Coeur de Lion and the ale brewed in Burton Abbey was famed for its excellence. Indeed it was the ale from this Abbey that was supplied to Mary, Queen of Scots, when she was imprisoned in Tutbury Castle in 1580.

It was not until the reign of George III however that the first commercial brewery was established at Burton by one Benjamin Printon. A few years later the owner of a cartage business decided that he would sooner make beer than cart it and so in 1777 he took over the brewery of Benjamin Printon. The carter's name was William Bass. It is very interesting to note that the present-day 'Bottle of Bass' largely owes its origin to an accident. In 1797 twenty years after the inception of the firm, the annual trade amounted to 2,000 barrels, a good proportion of which was exported to Russia, Finland and Poland, for in those days it was cheaper to send the beer by sea to Russia than by road to London!

This export trade, however, was practically eliminated in 1822 by a prohibitive tariff and so, looking round for other suitable markets Mr Bass decided to produce a pale ale suitable for the Far East. Unfortunately – or should it be fortunately? – a shipment on its way to India was wrecked in the Irish Channel and some of the salvaged casks of beer were sold in Liverpool. The quality of this special beer was so appreciated that the fame of 'East India Pale Ale' spread rapidly, with the result that it was soon put on the home market.

Two examples of India Pale Ale.

Above: McEwan's India Pale Ale.

Right: William Youngers India Pale Ale.

'Bass' is made using the finest quality barley soaked in cold water in steeping tanks for about 3 days. The water is then drained off and the barley is spread out in the malt house floor to allow germination to begin. When germination has progressed to the required degree the barley is moved to a kiln. This is a large room with a floor of finely perforated tiles through which heat can be brought to bear so arresting germination and at the same time drying the barley, which at this stage becomes known as malt. The malt is then sent to the brewery and fed into crushing mills.

The grist, as it is now called, is then mixed with hot water and run into mash tuns. Here it is allowed to infuse in exactly the same way that tea is made. Unlike tea, however, certain natural changes take place at this stage such as the starches being turned into malt sugars. When the infusion is completed the resultant clear liquid, known as wort, is run off. This process can be repeated; using the same grist in exactly the same way that a second pot of tea can be made from the first lot of tea leaves with exactly the same result that the second infusion is weaker than the first. It is, in fact, this second brew that was, in mediaeval times, known as 'small beer'.

After the wort has been run off, the mash tun is sprayed with water, or 'sparged' until all the extract is taken from the malt. And here it might be said the basic difference in brewing between the various grades and qualities of beer is purely a question of gravity. The stronger the beer and more malt and less water is used, and, conversely, for weaker beers, less malt and more water. Hops have no effect on gravity and are added in the proportions to the different brews as is required to attain the quality desired. From the mash tun the wort is run off into a large vessel known as an underback from which it is run into coppers where it is mixed with hops and boiled. The hops, until wanted, are stored in huge cold stores in which the temperature is kept at 2° of frost. On leaving the coppers the wort passes through a large vessel called a hop-back which is, in effect, a giant strainer which strains off the spent hops leaving the liquid clear again. The wort then runs into a cooler and through various refrigerators whereby it is cooled as rapidly as possible. Some aeration also takes place at this stage. From the refrigerators the wort flows into the fermentation vessels. Here, yeast is added and fermentation takes place, the yeast breaking down the malt sugars in the wort and converting them into alcohol.

Although many bottled beers are aerated with carbonic acid gas to give a sparkling drink with a good head, the effervescence found in a bottle of Bass is a completely natural process.

Such is the story of ale and beer, a story over 6,000 years old, a story, which is still being told and sung the world over … Cheers!

Enjoying a night out – Cheers!

ORIGINS OF PUB NAMES

Throughout Britain, many of the older Public Houses and hostelries are suffixed with the word; 'tavern', 'inn', 'hotel', 'vaults', 'house', 'arms' or 'head'.

In the past, a sharp distinction was drawn between the tavern and the inn as they were controlled by laws peculiar to each other, and held a different form of licence. The tavern was restricted to providing casual refreshment, both food and drink, and was usually kept by a vintner.

The inn was restricted to the receipt and entertainment of travellers and wayfarers by day and by night, along with the provision of accommodation.

Neither was allowed to overlap the other. The tavern was forbidden to harbour guests; the inn was forbidden to allow itself to be used for 'tippling' or as a place of idle resort. The tavern had to close at a certain hour, whereas the inn had to be open at all hours.

Today, there is no distinction between the two for the purpose of licensing, as it is widely accepted that their functions are much the same.

Nowadays, most inns, as part of their ordinary business provide the service given by the taverns of the past, and many taverns or public houses give the service that was once restricted to the inn.

The larger inns usually became 'hotels', the strict definition of which is an establishment providing accommodation and meals for travellers.

Other suffixes applied to public house names, along with their respective definitions include:

VAULTS: Meaning a room or space with arched walls and ceilings, especially underground, such as a cellar, basement or store-room.

HOUSE: A building having a particular function, or providing a particular service to the public.

ARMS: Heraldic bearings or insignia, as of a state, official, place, family or organisation.

HEAD: The upper end or extremity of something: Foremost in importance: Placed at the top or front.

The Langley Castle and Coburg Hotel, Coburg Terrace / Coburg Street, c.1918. The first pub is named after a castle in Northumberland and the second after the street on which it is located.

Beyond these definitions, the title or name of many public houses usually have a story behind them, the origin of which came about in 1393, when King Richard II of England compelled landlords to erect signs outside their premises. The legislation stated 'Whosoever shall brew ale in the town with intention of selling it must hang out a sign; otherwise he shall forfeit his ale.'

The reason for this was to make them easily visible to passing inspectors of the quality of the ale they provided (during this period, drinking water was not always good to drink and ale was the usual replacement).

Another important factor was that during the Middle Ages a large percentage of the population would have been illiterate and so pictures were more useful than words as a means of identifying a public house. For this reason there was often no reason to write the establishment's name on the sign and inns opened without a formal written name – the name being derived later from the illustration on the public house's sign. In this sense, a pub sign can be thought of as an early example of visual branding.

Instead of a painted sign, some publicans would identify their establishment by hanging or standing a distinctive object outside the pub such as a Boot, a Copper Kettle or a Crooked Billet (a branch from a tree).

In the modern era most British pubs still have highly decorated signs hanging over their doors, and these retain their original function of enabling the rapid identification of the public house – a memorable and prominently located pub sign is still an important means of picking up passing trade. Today's pub signs almost always bear the name of the pub, both in words and in pictorial representation.

Although the word 'The' appears on much public house signage, it is not considered to be an important part of the name. Likewise, the word 'Ye' should also be ignored as it is only another version of 'The', and alternative spellings such as 'Olde' is simply a derivation of a modern spelling.

Interesting, origins are not confined to old or traditional names, and some modern names are often nothing more than a marketing ploy frequently using amusing themes considered memorable, such as 'Slug and Lettuce'.

Elements of Pub names and their origins can be broken up into a relatively small number of categories, and so to provide a better understanding of this, some local examples are indicated and explained under the following appropriate headings:

BREWING RELATED

Barley Mow (Clive Street, North Shields).
Three Tuns (Wooden Bridge, North Shields).

HERALDRY

Heraldry was a fundamental element in naming pubs, and examples of items appearing on a Coat of Arms, would be:
Red Lion (Earsdon Village & Church Way, North Shields).
White Hart (Bedford Street, North Shields).
Three Bulls Heads (Union Street).

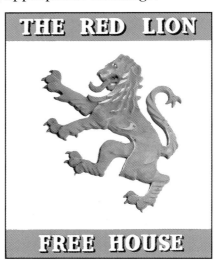

HISTORIC EVENTS

Saracen's Head (Liddell Street, North Shields).
Turk's Head (Duke Street & Linskill Street, North Shields and Front Street, Tynemouth).
Rose and Crown (Liddell Street & Tyne Street, North Shields).
Royal Oak (Bell Street & Mount Pleasant, North Shields).

HUNTING & BLOOD SPORTS

The Cock (Clive Street, North Shields).
Foxhunters (Preston North Road, Preston).
The Greyhound (Church Street, Bell Street, Toll Street & Bird Street, North Shields).
Falcon Arms (Dotwick Street).

LANDOWNERS

Many names with 'Arms' as a suffix, refer to the local land owner. This usually makes such names unique.

LOCATION

An 'Arms' name can also be derived from where the premises are situated, for example:
The Monkseaton Arms (Monkseaton) or **The Borough Arms** (Borough Road).

Likewise, the site of a pub can have a bearing on the name, such as:
Corner House (Bull Ring, North Shields). Standing on a corner or road junction.
Old Hundred (Albion Road, North Shields). At one time, the address was No.100 Albion Road.
High Point Hotel (The Promenade, Whitley Bay). Because of its prominent position, high on the seafront.

MYTHS & LEGENDS

Phoenix (Bedford Street, Clive Street & Earsdon Village).
Green Man (Liddell Street, North Shields).
Robin Hood (Front Street, Chirton & Murton Village).

OCCUPATIONS

Some 'Arms' signs refer to working occupations and on a similar basis to Heraldry and Trade Guilds they may indicate a trade or profession. Some examples are:

The Artillery Arms (Albion Road).	**The Masons Arms** (Bedford Street).
The Cordwainers Arms (Bell Street).	**The Mariners Arms** (Saville Street).

The Mariners Arms, the Sir Colin Campbell and the Ballarat Hotel, Saville Street West / Borough Road, c.1912.

PERSONAL NAMES OR TITLES

Marquis of Granby (Church Street, North Shields).
Prince of Wales (Liddell Street & Union Street, North Shields.
Lord Nelson (Camden Street, North Shields).
Shakespeare (Clive Street, Howard Street & Lishmans Quay, North Shields).
William Shakespeare, the English poet and playwright, had a number of inns named after him throughout the country.

PLACES

Tyne Inn (Camden Street & Tennyson Terrace, North Shields).
Northumberland Hotel (New Quay, North Shields & Percy Square, Tynemouth).
Raby Castle (Tyne Street, North Shields).
Alnwick Castle (Saville Street, North Shields).
Ballarat (Saville Street West, North Shields).
Fire Station (York Road, Whitley Bay).

PUNS & CORRUPTIONS

Although puns became increasingly popular through the 20th century, they should be considered with care. Supposed corruptions of foreign phrases usually have much simpler explanations, and many newer public houses have catchy names which are nothing other than a modern marketing strategy.

Bell and Bucket (Norfolk Street, North Shields).
Magic Lantern (Preston North Road, North Shields).
Sailors Return (Bell Street, North Shields).
Uncle Tom's Cabin (Bedford Street, North Shields).
Flower Pot (Albion Road West).
The Bedroom (Whitley Road, Whitley Bay).
Sammy Jacks (Front Street, Tynemouth).

Right: North Shields Fire Station, Norfolk Street, c.1957. This building later became the Bell and Bucket.

RELIGIOUS

Public Houses sometimes took their name from religious symbolism:
Anchor (Swans Quay/Duke Street & Bell Street, North Shields).
From the Bible passage (Hebrews 6:19): 'We have this as a sure and steadfast anchor of the soul, a hope.' This also relates to the derivation of the name Hope & Anchor.
Lamb (Dotwick Street, North Shields).
From John 1:29: 'Behold the Lamb of God, which taketh away the sins of the world.'
Salutation (Bell Street, North Shields & Front Street, Tynemouth).
The salute (by handshake) of the Archangel Gabriel to Mary when informing her she was to carry Jesus Christ.

ROYALTY

Royal names have always been popular (except under Oliver Cromwell's rule). It demonstrated the landlord's loyalty to authority (whether he was loyal or not) especially after the Restoration of the Monarchy when Richard Cromwell (Oliver's son) was sacked and Charles II was brought back from exile.

North Shields and the surrounding environs had its share of public houses here that were named after members of the Monarchy, and other items of royal symbolism.

Perhaps one of the most popular 'Royal' pub names in the United Kingdom is the **Queen Victoria**, named after the monarch at the time of greatest expansion of housing stock and associated public houses. She inspired great loyalty and affection, and publicans aimed to reflect this.

Examples of 'royal' pub names in the North Shields and surrounding areas are:
Kings Arms, Kings Head, Queens Head, Crown & Sceptre, Victoria, William IV etc.

SHIPS

Where the pub name is taken from the name of a ship.
Ship Hopewell (Duke Street, North Shields).
Ship Lady Jane (Bell Street).
Royal Sovereign (Bath Terrace, Tynemouth).

TRADES & TOOLS

Many trade names could also be derived from a heraldry source.
Carpenters Arms (Clive Street).
Cordwainers Arms (Bell Street).
Masons Arms (Ropery Bank, Stephenson Street & Bedford Street, North Shields).
Shipwrights Arms (Bell Street, Clive Street & Church Way, North Shields and Back Street, Tynemouth).
Shepherdess (Bell Street).
Post Boy (Stephenson Street, North Shields).
Plough (Dotwick Street, North Shields and Earsdon).

TRANSPORT

Rail: **The Station, The Railway, The Express.** (Usually pubs found close to a railway line or station.)
Road: **Waggon Inn, Coach & Horses, Pack Horse.**
Water: **Ferry, Ship, Brig, Corvette, Seine Boat, Navigation Tavern.**

TRADE GUILDS

It is worth noting that names beginning with the word 'Three' sometimes bear a close association with Heraldry, and can also be related to the Arms of some London livery companies or Trade Guilds:
Three Horseshoes (Chapel Lane, Monkseaton). The Farriers
Three Tuns (Wooden Bridge, North Shields). The Brewers and Vinters.

The Colonel Linskill, Charlotte Street, c.1905 – a pub named after a well known local landowner and dignitary.

EXTERNALLY TILED & DECORATED PUBS

During the early 1900s, a number of public houses were built and faced with glazed terracotta or decorated ceramic tiles, which were usually accompanied with the name of the establishment displayed in ornate signage and lettering.

There were a small number of pubs of this type in North Shields, and one in Tynemouth, which typically, had facades that were glazed in varying shades of brown, amber, and yellow, all of which added an attractive and prestigious style and appearance to the building. Although very hard wearing, this method of building was an exceptionally time consuming and expensive process to undertake. An architect would have to produce a finely detailed plan in order to prepare for the bricks and tiles to be individually manufactured, which in itself was a lengthy operation, as the finished items would also have to be checked to ensure they all fitted together perfectly. They would then,

The glazed facade of the Garricks Head, Saville Street.

in turn, have to be numbered before shipment to make certain that they were correctly constructed on site.

There were nine known local public houses in the North Shields area which had this style of faience, three of which have been demolished. Of the six remaining, only three were still trading as public houses in 2013, and are listed as follows:

1) **The Borough Arms**, Gardner Street, North Shields. (Demolished)
2) **The Crown & Sceptre**, Stephenson Street, North Shields. (Demolished)
3) **The Fountain Head**, Bedford Street, North Shields. (Demolished)
4) **The Berwick Arms**, Trinity Street, North Shields. (Closed)
5) **The Crane House**, Duke Street, North Shields. (Change of use / Preserved)
6) **The Railway**, Nile Street, North Shields. (Change of use / Conversion)
7) **The Cumberland Arms**, Front Street, Tynemouth. (Still Trading 2013)
8) **The Garricks Head**, Saville Street, North Shields. (Still Trading 2013)
9) **Tynemouth Lodge Hotel**, Tynemouth Road, North Shields. (Still Trading 2013)

Left: The Garricks Head, Saville Street, c.1928.

DIRECTORY OF NORTH SHIELDS PUBS, INNS & TAVERNS

Guide to using the Directory of Inns:

This directory contains a list of all the recorded ale houses, inns, taverns and public houses in North Shields High Town, Low Town and Bull Ring areas.

It does not include those premises on the outskirts or perimeter of the town, such as Chirton, Percy Main, Preston or Tynemouth. These areas will be covered in a separate edition of this book.

Notes:

1) All entries in this directory are alphabetic. To make searching simple, none of the establishment or premises names have been prefixed with the word: *'The'*.

2) The bold heading is the recorded or documented name of the establishment OR the name by which the premises were best known.

3) Some titles have been accompanied by a bracketed reference to premises of a different name. More information about the premises is available by following the bracketed name in the listing.

4) For the sake of consistency, premises which may have closed down temporarily and re-opened are considered to have been trading on a continuous basis. If this has been accompanied by a change of name, then this is reflected in the directory listing.

5) The address or street name shown is the location under which the premises were recorded. If more than one address or street name is shown, these are the subsequent addresses under which the premises have also been recorded over a period of years.

6) Any names shown in bold type in the accompanying narrative refer to other establishments which have also been included in this directory, and can be found by searching the alphabetical listing.

7) The *'First Record'* date shown at the end of each narrative indicates the year that the premises were first documented. This should be taken only as a general guide because the earliest available directory that I have been able to use to compile this book dates from 1822, and was used as a basic starting point. It is therefore apparent that many of the older premises showing a date of 1822 either existed or were established prior to that time.

8) The *'Last Record'* date shown at the end of the narrative indicates the year that the premises were last documented. Again, this should be taken only as a general guide. It is simply an indication of when the premises ceased to exist, whether through closure, conversion, demolition or lack of directory listings.

9) Where no *'First Record'* or *'Last Record'* date is shown, or is suffixed by *'Unconfirmed'*, this is because there is doubt, uncertainty or a possible conflict in the available information.

10) Where the *'Last Record'* includes the word *'Extant 2013'* – this means the premises were still in existence or still trading at the date of publication of this book.

The interior of the Albion Grill dining room, Norfolk Street, c.1935.

ABERDEEN ARMS

Clive Street *First Record: 1893 / Last Record: 1908*

ABERLLOLWYN ARMS

South Street / 27 Front Street
In 1895, Aberllolwyn Hall was recorded as a private residence within Llan-y-Chaiarn, a small parish and village in the county of Cardigan, 2 miles south of Aberystwyth.

There appear to be very few references to Aberllolwyn, and as there is no particular significance to the distinctly Welsh title given to the pub, the reason for such a name in North Shields is unknown.

The pub was situated on the south-eastern corner of South Street (Dock Road) and closed in 1932, before being demolished. *First Record: 1865 / Last Record: 1932*

ADMIRAL JERVIS

73 Bell Street
The **Admiral Jervis** is shown under this name on a map dated 1857, however it was later to become better known as the **Sun Inn**, and was a larger pub situated on the south side of Bell Street, standing opposite the foot of Fenwick's Bank Stairs, backing onto the River Tyne.

The pub was no doubt named after Admiral Sir John Jervis who served alongside Captain James Cook and General Wolfe at the siege of Quebec in 1759. In the French Wars, Jervis commanded the Mediterranean and Channel Fleets. He was known as a stern disciplinarian with a grim sense of humour. Admiral Jervis took command of the fleet at a time when, in his own words *"It was at the lowest ebb of licentiousness and ill discipline."* Through his own ruthless determination he transformed the fleet into a highly efficient fighting service. *First Record: 1857 / Last Record: 1887*

ADMIRAL NELSON

29 Liddell Street / 49 Liddell Street

Also known as the **Lord Nelson**, and named after the Naval Hero, this public house was situated on the bank side of Liddell Street, opposite the *Prince of Wales* tavern. *First Record: 1822 / Last Record: 1901*

ADMIRAL NELSON

69 George Street

Sometimes known as the **Lord Nelson**, this was the second of two public houses with this name in North Shields. *First Record: 1895 / Last Record: 1906*

ALBERT ARMS

6 Howard Street

The **Albert Arms** was a small pub near the foot of, and on the western side of Howard Street, just a few yards away from the Maritime Chambers Shipping Offices. The name was probably derived from Prince Albert, consort to Queen Victoria. *First Record: 1887 / Last Record: 1912*

ALBERT INN

18 Albert Terrace / 19 Albert Terrace / 142 Tynemouth Road The **Albert Inn** (*right, c.2010*) was situated on the corner of Albert Terrace, (Tynemouth Road) and North King Street. Albert Terrace is a sub-named street forming a short section of the north side of Tynemouth Road, between North Church Street & North King Street. It is likely that both the street and inn were named in honour of Queen Victoria's consort, Prince Albert. The premises ceased trading and closed in October 2012. *First Record: 1887 / Last Record: 2012*

ALBION GRILL

(Refer to: **ALBION HOTEL**)
23 Norfolk Street / 72 Saville Street

ALBION HOTEL

23 Norfolk Street / 72 Saville Street
The imposing **Albion Hotel** (*left, c.1961*) was one of the largest High Town buildings, and stood on Norfolk Street at the eastern end of Saville Street, facing west. The adjoining assembly rooms were founded in 1853 as part of the hotel.

In 1884 the **Albion Hotel** was demolished, which allowed Saville Street to become a continuous thoroughfare and connect with Lower Pearson Street. This road later became known as Charlotte Street. The remaining Assembly Rooms were then remodelled to incorporate the **Albion Hotel**, on the corner site where it later became known as the **Albion Grill**. The premises closed down during the 1970s and were destroyed by a large fire in 1985. It was demolished shortly afterwards. *First Record: 1850 / Last Record: 1985*

ALBION INN

30 Nile Street /
17 Albion Road
The word 'Albion' is an archaic name for Great Britain and the **Albion Inn** (*right, c.1962*) was probably named after the road on which it stands, ie; Albion Road. Located on the south-west corner of Albion Road and Nile Street, the pub was locally nicknamed and referred to as the **Top**

House. This name was later adopted to become the official name for the pub and the name 'Albion' was dropped. *First Record: 1887 / Last Record: Extant 2013*

ALNWICK CASTLE

26 Saville Street / 28 Saville Street / 22 Church Way / 112 Church Way
The **Alnwick Castle** (*below, c.1930*) is one of the oldest established public houses still

in existence in North Shields and occupied a prominent site on the south side of Saville Street, at the corner of Church Way. The structure has barely been altered from its original shape, format and design.

In January 2005, the famous and long established name was changed for a short time to the **Teac Fiddlers** when new owners took over the building in an effort to upgrade its status by converting the premises to style it as a theme bar. The name was short lived when it reverted back to its original title of the **Alnwick Castle**.
First Record: 1834 / Last Record: Extant 2013

ANCHOR TAVERN

Swans Quay / Clive Street / 14 Duke Street / 18 Duke Street
Locally referred to as the **Foul Anchor** and the **Raffled Anchor**, this tavern was situated on Swans Quay, (between Clive Street and the River Tyne), adjacent to the very narrow Hole-in-the-Wall Quay at the rear.

The anchor has obvious connections with shipping in a busy North Shields riverside port, however the origins were probably derived from religious symbolism, after the Bible passage (Hebrews 6:19): *'Which Hope we have as an Anchor of the soul, both sure and stedfast, and which entereth into that within the veil.'*
First Record: 1834 / Last Record: 1897

ANGEL HOTEL (Refer to: VICTORIA HOTEL)

Albion Street
This pub was situated next door to the **Victoria Hotel**, and just prior to 1897, the two buildings were combined to became the **Ye Olde Hundred**.
*First Record: 1822-1897 as the **Angel Hotel** / Last Record: 1897 to become **Ye Olde Hundred***

AQUATIC ARMS

1 William Street / 76 Rudyerd Street

The **Aquatic Arms** (*right, c.1964*) was situated on the corner of William Street and Rudyerd Street and closed down as a public house in the 1970s. The building was converted to become a retail shop. *First Record: 1864 / Last Record: 1970s*

ARK

22 Saville Street

Biblical references to the Ark suggest the unusual name for this public house of which nothing is known. *First Record: 1822 / Last Record: 1834*

ARTILLERY ARMS

2 Albion Road

Military undertones probably lend the name to this public house which stood on the corner of Albion Road and Norfolk Street. *First Record: 1867 / Last Record: 1960s*

BALLARAT HOTEL

42 Saville Street West / 13 Borough Road

One of the more well known hostelries in North Shields for many years was the

Ballarat Hotel (*right, c.1910*), which occupied a site on the south-east corner of Saville Street West and Borough Road.

Often nicknamed 'The Rat', it derived its name from the town of Ballarat, in the state of Victoria, Australia, soon after the great rush to the Ballarat Goldfields during the mid 1800s. It is generally accepted that the origin of the name came from two aboriginal words; 'Balla' and 'Arat', signifying a resting or camping place. *First Record: 1887 / Last Record: 2010*

BALMORAL CASTLE

4 Stephenson Street

A Royal connection is evident with the name of Balmoral.
First Record: Unconfirmed / Last Record: Unconfirmed

BALMORAL HOUSE

Church Street *First Record: 1895 / Last Record: 1905*

BACKWORTH ARMS

Liddell Street

No apparent connection with the local village of Backworth.
First Record: 1892 / Last Record: 1906

BARLEY MOW

Clive Street

The **Barley Mow** is not an uncommon name for a public house, and the name is derived from part of the brewing process. Barley is laid in a malting, heated and watered until the grain germinates. The grain is then cooked which kills the germination process and the result is called malt. Malt is the ingredient in beer which gives it its sweet taste and colour. The 'mow' is a type of stack. Its exact location on Clive Street is unconfirmed. *First Record: 1827 / Last Record: 1827*

BAY HORSE

Clive Street / Bay Horse Quay

The **Bay Horse** was situated just off Clive Street, near the end of Bay Horse Quay, and backed directly onto the River Tyne. *First Record: 1822 / Last Record: 1887*

BAY HORSE

39 Duke Street / Ferryboat Landing

This was the second of two public houses bearing this name in North Shields, and was situated next to the riverside near to the ferry landing on Duke Street; the **Bay Horse** was accessed via an alleyway situated between the **Steam Ferry House** and the **Sussex Arms**. *First Record: 1834 / Last Record: 1855*

BEDFORD ARMS (Refer to: DUKE OF BEDFORD)

65 Bedford Street

BEDFORD HOTEL (Refer to: PHOENIX TAVERN & FOUNTAIN HEAD)

91 Bedford Street *First Record: 1887 / Last Record: 1887*

BEE HIVE INN

12 Dotwick Street / 31 Dotwick Street

Smaller than the neighbouring **Clarendon Hotel**, The **Bee Hive Inn** (*right, c.1898*) was situated a little further south, on the west side of Dotwick Street. It has long since been demolished. *First Record: 1822 / Last Record: 1899*

BELL AND BUCKET

Norfolk Street

The fine stone building on the East side of Norfolk Street, which is now the **Bell and Bucket**, was originally the Union British School which first opened in 1840. By 1906 it had been converted to accommodate North Shields Fire Brigade which remained here until 1959.

The building was converted to a public house in 1986, with the unusual and catchy name being derived from its former use as a Fire Station.
First Record: 1986 / Last Record: Extant 2013

BERWICK ARMS

1 Trinity Street / 2 Trinity Terrace / 2 Coach Lane

The **Berwick Arms** (*below, c.2009*) was situated on the north corner of Coach Lane and Trinity Street. Externally, this building was probably the most decorative of all the public houses in North Shields, as the external façade construction consists of ornate glazed coloured brickwork and terracotta tiles. It was one of just a small number of public houses in North Shields faced in this style. The building closed in 2010 and converted into a private dwelling house. *First Record: 1887 / Last Record: c.2010*

BETTY BADDOO (Refer to: MARINERS ARMS)

1 Saville Street West

BIRD

Clive Street
*First Record: 1847 /
Last Record: 1847*

BLACK BOY

Clive Street *First Record: 1834 / Last Record: 1834*

BLACK BULL

Bull Ring / Collingwood Street *First Record: 1822 / Last Record: 1827*

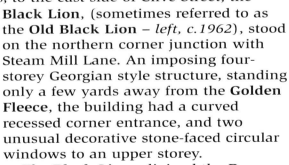

BLACK BULL INN (Refer to: GREEN MAN)

14 Liddell Street / 15 Liddell Street / 22 Liddell Street / Pandon Bank

BLACK COCK

Clive Street / Black Cock Quay *First Record: 1822 / Last Record: 1834*

BLACK LION

5 Clive Street / 38 Clive Street / 40 Clive Street / Steam Mill Lane

Situated directly opposite Britannia Bank Stairs, to the east side of Clive Street, the

Black Lion, (sometimes referred to as the **Old Black Lion** – *left, c.1962*), stood on the northern corner junction with Steam Mill Lane. An imposing four-storey Georgian style structure, standing only a few yards away from the **Golden Fleece**, the building had a curved recessed corner entrance, and two unusual decorative stone-faced circular windows to an upper storey.

The **Black Lion** adjoined the **Percy Arms**, which stood on Steam Mill Lane, the cobbles of which are still evident behind the **Golden Fleece** (later to be re-named as the **Porthole**).

Having existed since at least 1850, the **Black Lion** was still open in 1964, before being demolished in 1967 to make way for a new building, which was to become The North Eastern Rubber Company.

First Record: 1822 / Last Record: 1964

BLACK SWAN INN

93 Bell Street / Bland Square

The **Black Swan Inn**, situated on the south side of Bell Street, extended southwards towards the River Tyne. The premises had an extensive frontage of about 65 feet, with a timber-built gallery beyond, and a river frontage of about 40 feet, and the west side of the building overlooked Bland Square. It was first mentioned in an abstract of deeds dated February 1690.

The basement comprised two vaulted cellars under the bar, with a large ceiled cellar extending towards the river. The ground floor, consisted of a large bar, sitting room, snug, club room (with a gallery outside overlooking the river), a kitchen and W.C. To the first floor, there were three bedrooms, a sitting room, bathroom and numerous large closets, with twelve other large rooms within the property. A further gallery was used in connection with the cellarage, fitted with a crane, which was able to lift up to a ton in weight. The **Black Swan** could also be accessed from the river, via a passage to the left of the building, adjacent to Lambs Quay and Maitlands Lane. This passage also gave access to Bell Street. *First Record: 1690 / Last Record: 1903*

The Black Swan Inn (centre of the picture with the timber gallery), Bell Street / Bland Square, c.1900.

BLACKSMITHS ARMS

34 Liddell Street *First Record: 1886 / Last Record: 1886*

BLUE BELL

46 Bell Street

The **Blue Bell** was one of the larger public houses on Bell Street, and it was situated on the north side of the road, immediately next to the foot of the High Lighthouse Stairs. *First Record: 1855 / Last Record: 1930*

BLUE BELL

Bull Ring / Collingwood Street
First Record: Unconfirmed / Last Record: Unconfirmed

BLUE BELL INN
Belle Vue Terrace
Prior to 1822, a **Blue Bell Inn** is recorded, which is known to have stood in fields, on the site of what is now the present Belle Vue Terrace, Coach Lane. No other information or details are known about this inn. *First Record: Unconfirmed / Last Record: Pre-1822*

BLYTH AND TYNE HOTEL
1 Charlotte Street / 1 Lower Pearson Street / Stephenson Street
One of many corner site public houses in North Shields, the **Blyth & Tyne Hotel** was situated on the north-east corner of Charlotte Street and Stephenson Street. *First Record: 1887 / Last Record: 1940*

BLYTH HOUSE
Clive Street
Facing Clive Street, from the east side of the road, the **Blyth House** was situated between Scarp Landing and Skipsey's Quay. *First Record: Unconfirmed / Last Record: Unconfirmed*

BOARD
New Quay *First Record: 1834 / Last Record: 1834*

BOARD INN
Clive Street
The **Board Inn** was probably the smallest of all the inns and taverns in North Shields Low Town. It stood on the west side of Clive Street opposite the **Star & Garter Inn**, where Wascoe's Bank Stairs separated it from the **Londonderry Arms** which stood next door to the south. *First Record: 1834 / Last Record: 1834*

BOARD INN
34 Tyne Street
This was the third similarly named public house in North Shields. **The Board** was a relatively common title for an inn in the UK, and the name may have been derived from its possible use as a lodging house. *First Record: 1847 / Last Record: 1847*

BOARS HEAD
Clive Street / Broad Quay *First Record: 1822 / Last Record: 1834*

BOILERMAKERS ARMS
12 Wellington Street
This pub was situated on the south-east corner of Wellington Street and Little Bedford Street. *First Record: 1886 / Last Record: 1886*

BOROUGH ARMS
29 Camden Street / 61 Camden Street
Also known as **Ye Olde Boro' Arms**, this was a small pub, situated on the west side of Camden Street. After demolition, the site was occupied by part of the car park and access areas of the North Shields Shopping Centre Mall to the rear of the present Central Library. The name is likely to have been chosen to mark the charter of incorporation of North Shields in 1849. *First Record: 1850 / Last Record: 1940*

BOROUGH ARMS
2 Borough Road / 26 Gardner Street / 28 Gardner Street
The second public house by the name of the **Borough Arms** was situated on the north-east corner of Borough Road Bank and Gardner Street. It was one of a small number of public houses in the area which retained the original glazed terracotta faience and pub signage above the windows and entrance. *First Record: 1865 / Last Record: 1940*

BREWERS ARMS (Refer to: BREWERY ARMS)
Beacon Street

BREWERY ARMS
Beacon Street
Also known as the **Brewers Arms** and **Brewery House**, this building stood on the western side of Beacon Street. It virtually backed onto the nearby **Oak Tavern** which stood on nearby Charlotte Street. *First Record: 1850 / Last Record: 1855*

BREWERY HOUSE (Refer to: BREWERY ARMS)
Beacon Street

BREWERY INN
2 Bull Ring
The **Brewery Inn** stood on the east side of the Bull Ring between the **Bull Ring Inn** and the **Essex Arms**. *First Record: 1887 / Last Record: 1899*

BRIDGE INN (Refer to: PUSH & PULL INN)
3 Bedford Street

BRITANNIA
Clive Street *First Record: 1822 / Last Record: 1834*

BRITANNIA INN (Refer to: BRITANNIA VAULTS)
12 Church Street

BRITANNIA VAULTS
12 Church Street
The **Britannia Vaults**, also known as the **Britannia Inn**, stood halfway between Charlotte Street and Tyne Street, on the east side of Church Street, diagonally opposite the **Kings Head**. *First Record: 1865 / Last Record: 1920*

BULL RING INN
3 Bull Ring / 10 Bull Ring
The **Bull Ring Inn**, (which was later to become the **New Bull Ring Inn**), stood in the south-west corner of the Bull Ring, close to the **Dock Inn**, and separated by Grey Horse Quay. There have been three pubs of this name built on the same site, all of which have long since disappeared. *First Record: 1822 / Last Record: 1930*

BURDON ARMS (Refer to: BURDON MAIN)
Duke Street / Dotwick Street

BURDON MAIN
Duke Street / Dotwick Street
The **Burdon Main** or **Burdon Arms** is recorded in directories as being situated on both Duke Street and Dotwick Street. These streets were only a short distance apart in the Bull Ring area of North Shields so it is probable that this is the same public house. *First Record: 1822 / Last Record: 1865*

BURTON HOUSE (Refer to: SHAKESPEARE TAVERN)
Howard Street / 41 Tyne Street / News Room Bank

BURNS HEAD (Refer to: BURNS TAVERN)
Clive Street / Bell Street / Custom House Quay / Broad Quay

BURNS TAVERN
Clive Street / Bell Street / Custom House Quay / Broad Quay
Collectively known as the **Burns Tavern**, the **Burns Head**, the **Robert Burns Tavern**

and the **Robbie Burns Inn**, it was named after the famous Scottish Poet (1759-96). This inn was hidden away from view, and situated between Broad Quay and Skipsey's Quay, at the eastern end of Clive Street, near Wooden Bridge. The back of the building faced the River Tyne. *First Record: 1822 / Last Record: 1899*

CAMDEN ARMS
12 Camden Street *First Record: 1865 / Last Record: 1865*

CANNON INN
14 North Street / Milburn Place *First Record: 1893 / Last Record: 1906*

CARPENTERS ARMS
Clive Street / Skipp's Quay
First Record: 1822 / Last Record: 1827

CASK & STILLAGE
(Refer to: **WHITE HART**)
Bedford Street

CENTRAL ARMS
6 Saville Street West
First Record: 1938 / Last Record: 1938

CENTURIAN ARMS
Bull Ring / Collingwood Street
The **Centurian** was a large building on the Bull Ring, dominating a corner site at the north end of Dotwick Street. To the rear, the building adjoined the **Dock House**, at the corner of Dotwick Street and Dock Lane. *First Record: 1834 / Last Record: 1865*

CHAIN LOCKER
(Refer to **CRANE HOUSE**)
44 Duke Street / 50 Duke Street

CITY OF DUBLIN
72 Tyne Street
Located on the bank side of Tyne Street, the **City of Dublin** stood almost opposite the foot of Norfolk Street. *First Record: 1887 / Last Record: 1887*

The Chain Locker (formerly the Crane House), Duke Street, c.2004.

CLARENDON HOTEL
35 Dotwick Street / 36 Dotwick Street
The **Clarendon Hotel** was a large building which stood to the west side of Dotwick Street, opposite the head of one of the huge Graving Docks.

An Ordnance Survey map dated 1857 indicates that the hotel occupied the site of two earlier public houses; the **Hylton Castle** and the **Vulcans Arms**. The pub was probably named after George William Frederick Villiers, 4th Earl of Clarendon (1800-70), a British statesman who was ambassador to Spain during the Carlist war and then Lord Privy Seal. As Lord Lieutenant of Ireland, he made efforts to ease disorder and distress during the famine and was Foreign Secretary (1853-58) during the Crimean War. *First Record: 1887 / Last Record: 1899*

CLOCK TAVERN (Refer to: **CLOCK VAULTS**)
4 Toll Street / Toll Square

CLOCK VAULTS

4 Toll Street / Toll Square
Originally known as the **Clock Tavern**, the **Clock Vaults** was situated on Toll Street, near to the corner with Toll Square. *First Record: 1855 / Last Record: 1930*

CLOCK VAULTS

30 Bedford Street / 33 Wellington Street / 34 Wellington Street
As the second public house by this name in North Shields, the well known **Clock Vaults** (*below, c.1964*) was one of the larger premises in the High Town, and was an

imposing building which stood on the south-east corner of Bedford Street and Wellington Street. *First Record: 1887 / Last Record: 1968*

COACH AND HORSES

Duke Street / 20 Bull Ring
First Record: 1822 / Last Record: 1834

COAL WAGGON

Chorlton Place
First Record: 1827 / Last Record: 1827

COBLE BOAT (Refer to: COBLE INN)

19 Bell Street / 33 Bell Street / Coble Entry

COBLE INN

19 Bell Street / 33 Bell Street / Coble Entry
The **Coble Inn**, or **Coble Boat** as it was sometimes known, was situated on the northern side of Bell Street next to Coble Entry, which led up the bank side to Tyne Street via Ropery Lane and Ropery Stairs. *First Record: 1834 / Last Record: 1899*

COBOURG HOTEL

1 Coburg Street / 18 Coburg Street / 20 Coburg Terrace / 21 Coburg Terrace
Also known simply as the **Coburg** (originally and probably incorrectly spelled Cobourg), the building was situated on the corner of Coburg Terrace, (Tynemouth Road) and Coburg Street. Coburg Terrace is a sub-named street forming a short section of the north side of Tynemouth Road, between North King Street and Coburg Street.

The name Coburg was probably derived from Queen Victoria's connection with Prince Albert who descended from the German House of Saxe-Coburg and Gotha. During the 1990s, the **Coburg** was renamed as the **Mash Tun**, in an effort to

An advert for the Coburg Hotel.

renew the image, however it proved an unpopular choice, and reverted to its original name a short time afterwards.

The premises ceased trading as a public house in 2011 and converted to become a retail mini-supermarket. *First Record: 1887 / Last Record: 2011*

COCK TAVERN
27 Clive Street
Cock-fighting was prevalent in the early 1800s, and it is possible that this pub name may have derived its name from a connection with the sport.
First Record: 1822 / Last Record: 1850

COLLINGWOOD MAIN
North Street *First Record: 1827 / Last Record: 1827*

COLLINGWOOD TAVERN
1 Bell Street *First Record: 1847 / Last Record: 1847*

COLONEL LINSKILL
17 Charlotte Street / 34 Charlotte Street / 35 Charlotte Street
The name of the Linskill family has long been associated with North Shields, and it is probable that this pub took its name from Colonel William Linskill, who was the High Sheriff of Northumberland in 1806.

According to the Ordnance Survey Town Plan of 1896, the original **Colonel Linskill** inn stood on the north side of Charlotte Street between King Street and Reed Street, however, over the years, these streets were either changed, lost to development, or renamed, so the original description of the location may be no longer applicable or valid. The original pub was demolished and rebuilt on the same site in 1937, so the **Colonel Linskill**, was therefore situated on Charlotte Street, on the corner of Kettlewell Terrace.

In 1986, the pub was renamed as the **Fog on the Tyne** in an effort to try and renew what was then a somewhat tarnished image. The name was derived from a popular song title of the era, by the local pop group; *'Lindisfarne'*. This change seemed to have little effect,

The Colonel Linskill, Charlotte Street, c.2002.

and so it underwent a further name change in October 1992 to the **Laurel Arms** in yet another attempt to rejuvenate the pub. This time, the name change was dedicated to Stan Laurel, of the famous Laurel and Hardy comedy duo, who was once resident in nearby Dockwray Square during the early 1900s.

Neither of these changes had any significant effect as the pub continued to be referred to as *'The Linskill'*, and so it reverted back to its original name just a few years later. *First Record: 1834 / Last Record: Extant 2013*

COMMERCIAL HOTEL (& POSTING HOUSE)
Howard Street
The **Commercial Hotel** was a large building situated on the east side of Howard Street, close to the end of Union Street. *First Record: 1822 / Last Record: 1865*

CORDWAINERS ARMS

Bell Street

The term cordwainer has generally fallen out of use from the English language; however a cordwainer (or cordovan) is somebody who makes shoes or other articles from fine soft leather. The word is derived from 'cordwain', or 'cordovan'; the leather produced in Cordoba, Spain. It is open to speculation why the **Cordwainers Arms** was so named. *First Record: 1822 / Last Record: 1827*

CORNER HOUSE

Bull Ring *First Record: 1827 / Last Record: 1827*

CORPORATION ARMS

125 Linskill Street / 126 Linskill Street / 127 Linskill Street

The first of two public houses recorded under this name in North Shields from the mid 1800s. *First Record: 1851 / Last Record 1940*

CORPORATION ARMS

9 Wellington Street

The **Corporation Arms** stood on the western corner of Wellington Street and Church Way. In 1834-55 and 1857-1940, it was recorded as the **Wellington House** or **Wellington Hotel**. *First Record: 1855 / Last Record: 1855*

CORVETTE

Charlotte Street / Beacon Street

The **Corvette** stood at the eastern end of Charlotte Street, at the north-west corner of Beacon Street and Bird Street. It was built in 1958, close to the site of the earlier **Robin Hood** pub. In later years, the **Corvette** fell into decline, and was demolished in the mid 1990s. A corvette is a small, manoeuvrable, lightly armed warship, and was probably just a modern-day name allocated to the pub when it was built as there appears to be no other significance. *First Record: 1958 / Last Record: Mid 1990s*

The Robin Hood Inn and the Corvette, Beacon Street, c.1958.

COTTAGE OF INDUSTRY (Refer to: INDUSTRY)

Coble Dene Bank

COUNTY HOTEL (Refer to: EUROPEAN AND UNITED STATES)

5 Railway Terrace / 11 Railway Terrace

CRANE HOUSE

44 Duke Street / 50 Duke Street

Situated on the west side of Duke Street, near to the present ferry landing stage, the **Crane House** was a corner building believed to have been named after a dockside crane, a picture of which was incorporated within the original glasswork of the premises. The **Crane House** has stood on this site since at least 1850, however it was rebuilt in 1905 from a design by Joseph Oswald and Son, and although known as the **Crane House Vaults** it was renamed as the **Crane Hotel**. Previously owned by W.H. Allison & Co., Wine & Spirit Merchants and Brewers, of North Shields, the premises came into the possession of Newcastle Breweries on its formation in 1890.

The new building was styled in brown glazed brickwork on the lower level, and was one of a small number of public houses in the area which retained the original glazed terracotta faience. Internally, there was a front bar with a rear sitting room, served by a single bar counter, with a hatch to the rear room.

In the early 1900s, the **Crane House** was the last building in Duke Street, a narrow street which led to the rear of the docks to the south via the Bull Ring. By the end of the First World War, most of the buildings on the south side of Duke Street had been demolished, but the **Crane House** managed to survive, standing alone at the end of the New Quay.

Latterly, the pub underwent a name change on a nautical theme to be known as the **Chain Locker**, but in 2004 it closed the doors as a public house for the last time, and with its remaining listed frontage, it

The Crane Hotel, Duke Street, c.1910.

was incorporated into a new housing development where its heritage was preserved.
First Record: 1834 / Last Record: 2004

CRANE HOUSE VAULTS / CRANE HOTEL (Refer to: CRANE HOUSE)

44 Duke Street / 50 Duke Street *First Record: 1905 / Last Record: 2004*

CRESCENT TAVERN

83 Hudson Street *First Record: 1822 / Last Record: 1940*

CRITERION

11 Tyne Street / 12 Tyne Street

Also known as the **Criterion Restaurant**, this pub was situated on the north side of Tyne Street, and stood between the junctions with Norfolk Street and Stephenson Street. *First Record: 1887 / Last Record: 1940*

CROWN

Beacon Street

The first of three pubs recorded with this name in North Shields.
First Record: 1850 / Last Record: 1850

CROWN

7 Camden Street / 19 Camden Street

The **Crown**, was a small building which stood on the west side of Camden Street, a little to the south of its junction with Saville Street, on the area now occupied by a supermarket. *First Record: 1855 / Last Record: 1865*

CROWN INN

30 Clive Street

The **Crown Inn** stood on the west side of Clive Street, adjacent to the New Quay Stairs and opposite the **Golden Fleece**. The **Crown** was demolished in the late 1800s to make way for St. Peter's Church which was built on the corner of Clive Street and Borough Road Bank. *First Record: 1850 / Last Record: 1855*

CROWN AND ANCHOR

Clive Street

Situated on the east side of Clive Street, the **Crown and Anchor** adjoined the Hole in the Wall Quay to the north. *First Record: 1855 / Last Record: 1855*

CROWN AND CUSHION

44 Liddell Street

The **Crown and Cushion** was situated on the south side of Liddell Street, directly opposite the **Green Man (Black Bull Inn)** and the foot of Green Man Bank. *First Record: 1850 / Last Record: 1865*

CROWN AND SCEPTRE

29 Stephenson Street / 184 Stephenson Street, Demolished in the late 1970s the **Crown and Sceptre** stood on the west side of Stephenson Street, close to the junction with Saville Street. Until its demolition, the **Crown & Sceptre** (*right, c.1960*) was one of a small number of public houses in the area which retained the original glazed terracotta faience and pub signage above the windows and entrance. *First Record: 1850 / Last Record: 1979*

CROWN AND THISTLE

41 Duke Street

The **Crown and Thistle** stood on the west side of Duke Street, adjacent to Kirby's Bank Stairs, and adjoined the **Crane House Vaults**. *First Record: 1822 / Last Record: 1855*

CRYSTAL TAVERN

43 Hudson Street *First Record: 1867 / Last Record: 1867*

CUMBERLAND ARMS

27 Liddell Street / 40 Liddell Street

The **Cumberland Arms** or **Cumberland House** as it was sometimes known, stood on the south side of Liddell Street, opposite the bottom of Pandon Bank. The inn adjoined the **Trawlers Arms**. *First Record: 1850 / Last Record: 1865*

CUMBERLAND ARMS

Low Lights

This is probably the same premises as those recorded above on Liddell Street. *First Record: 1865 / Last Record: 1865*

CUMBERLAND HOUSE (Refer to: CUMBERLAND ARMS)

27 Liddell Street / 40 Liddell Street

CUSTOM HOUSE TAVERN

Bell Street / Union Quay
The **Custom House Tavern** was a small building which stood on the south side of the road, at the eastern end of Bell Street, directly next to Union Quay.
First Record: 1850 / Last Record: 1865

CUSTOMS

83 Hudson Street *First Record: 1865 / Last Record: 1865*

CYPRUS

24 Clive Street
The **Cyprus Inn** was one of the very small Low Town inns, and stood on the east side of Clive Street, between Swan's Quay and Steel's Quay. *First Record: 1887 / Last Record: 1899*

DOCK HOTEL

(Refer to **DOCK HOUSE**)
16 Liddell Street / 23 Liddell Street /
42 Liddell Street

DOCK HOTEL

Northumberland Dock
The **Dock Hotel**, or **Dock House**, was located near Northumberland Dock, and has existed since the 1870s.

The house was run by members of the Beck family since that time, and locally, the pub has always known as 'Minnie Becks'. The original licensee was a William Gibson, followed in the 1920s by his daughter, Jane Beck, and subsequently in 1942 by her daughter, Mary Ann Beck, (affectionately and locally known as Minnie Beck). Minnie Beck ran the pub in the name of her brother, George. Throughout its lifespan, the **Dock Hotel** (*above, c.1930*) had no licence to sell wines or spirits and was purely a typical old ale house, however Minnie bent the rules, by serving spirits from under the counter, and managed to evade prosecution during her term as landlady, by simply being a firm judge of who had had enough to drink.

Minnie Beck was a teetotaller, who would refuse to serve anyone she did not know, or whom she did not like, and rather than allow rowdiness, she would simply close the house. Aged 86 in July 1973, the pub closed after Minnie was attacked and savagely beaten in her bedroom following a burglary. The **Dock Hotel** was demolished in 1974, during the time that Minnie was hospitalised, but she never fully recovered, and died in 1976. *First Record: c.1870 / Last Record: 1974*

DOCK HOUSE

16 Liddell Street / 23 Liddell Street / 42 Liddell Street
The **Dock House**, also known as the **Dock Hotel**, was only a small building, which was situated at the commencement of the narrowest part of the road on the south side of Liddell Street. The pub was neighbour to the **Trawlers Arms** next door, with the larger **Green Man (Black Bull Inn)** opposite. *First Record: 1822 / Last Record: 1899*

DOCK HOUSE (Refer to: DOCK HOTEL)

Northumberland Dock

DOCK HOUSE

Dotwick Street
The **Dock House** was a large building which stood on the corner of Dotwick Street and Dock Lane, and adjoined the **Centurian** public house to the north.
First Record: 1850 / Last Record: 1855

DOCK INN

60 North Street

The fourth of a number of similarly named pubs in North Shields beginning with the term 'Dock' because of the nearby connection with shipping. The **Dock Inn**, later to become the **New Dock Inn** was situated on the north-west corner of North Street, at its junction with East Street, in the area referred to as Mount Pleasant. It is likely that it derived its name from the opening of the nearby Smith's Docks in 1852.

First Record: 1855 / Last Record: 1940

The Dock Inn, North Street, c.1912.

DUKE OF BEDFORD

65 Bedford Street / 115 Bedford Street

The **Duke of Bedford** was situated on the west side of Bedford Street, just a few yards north of the junction with West Percy Street. The name of Bedford is derived from the Russell line of peerage, popularised since the 15th century, (with the nearby Russell Street also having an obvious connection to the peerage name). The building was later converted to a shop after its closure as a pub. *First Record: 1850 / Last Record: 1940*

DUKE OF EDINBURGH

9 Upper Pearson Street / 102 Church Street

The **Duke of Edinburgh** was a large building which stood at the north-east corner of Upper Pearson Street and Church Street. The name for the pub had no doubt been chosen because the title at this time had been conferred on Prince Alfred, second son of Queen Victoria. This site is now occupied by part of North Shields Police Station.

First Record: 1887 / Last Record: 1940

DUKE OF PORTLAND

Collingwood Street

The Duke of Portland is a peerage title created in 1716 for Henry Bentinck, who was already the Earl of Portland. The Dukedom of Portland became extinct on the 9th Duke's death, in 1990, though the 9th Duke's distant cousin succeeded him as Earl of Portland. The ducal seat was Welbeck Abbey, Nottinghamshire.

There is no obvious reason as to why a public house in North Shields was given this name. The exact location is unconfirmed *First Record: 1834 / Last Record: 1834*

DUKE OF SUSSEX

43 Church Street / 45 Church Street / 80 Church Street

The **Duke of Sussex** public house stood on the eastern corner of Church Street at its junction with Upper Pearson Street. The name was simply a peerage title first created in 1801, for the sixth son of George III. *First Record: 1850 / Last Record: 1940*

DUKE OF WELLINGTON

55 Church Way

Situated on the west side of Church Way, the **Duke of Wellington** was a small building, located a little to the north of its junction with Wellington Street, on which the name has a bearing. The name was attributed to Arthur Wellesley, 1st Duke of Wellington in 1814. *First Record: 1850 / Last Record: 1855*

DUKE OF YORK
15 King Street
Situated towards the bottom of, and on the eastern side of King Street, during the mid 1800s the **Duke of York** was one of the larger pubs of the High Town. The Duke of York has generally been recognised as a title of Nobility which has been given to the second son of a monarch since the 15th century. *First Record: 1822 / Last Record: 1930*

DUNDEE ARMS
Union Road
An unknown significance in the name of this pub. *First Record: 1834 / Last Record: 1834*

DUTALIA HOTEL
Clive Street / Steel's Quay
Situated off Clive Street to the east, the **Dutalia Hotel** overlooked the River Tyne on Steel's Quay, adjoining the **Lindsay Arms**. The origin of the name 'Dutalia' has not been ascertained. *First Record: Unconfirmed / Last Record: Unconfirmed*

EAGLE INN
9 Upper Pearson Street
The **Eagle Inn** stood in a prominent corner position at the south-east corner of Upper Pearson Street and Upper Church Street. *First Record: 1855 / Last Record: 1865*

EAGLE TAVERN
Bland Square
First Record: 1847 / Last Record: 1847

EAGLE
Skipseys' Quay
One of three similarly named public houses recorded in North Shields.
First Record: 1850 / Last Record: 1850

EARL GREY
15 Hudson Street / 16 Hudson Street
Probably named as such in common with another nearby North Shields public house. *First Record: 1850 / Last Record: 1938*

The Earl Grey, Hudson Street, c.1935.

EARL GREY INN
27 Linskill Street / 53 Linskill Street / 14 Lower Pearson Street / 103 Charlotte Street / 104 Charlotte Street
The **Earl Grey Inn** was a corner building, situated on the east side of Linskill Street at the junction with Lower Pearson Street (later Charlotte Street). The premises were probably named after Charles Grey, (Second Earl Grey 1764–1845), a British politician who as Prime Minister (1830-34) implemented parliamentary and social reforms, notably the abolition of slavery throughout the British Empire.
First Record: 1834 / Last Record: 1940

EARL PERCY
Stephenson Street
This public house is likely to have derived its name from Algernon George Percy, 6th Duke of Northumberland, KG, (1810-99) who was styled Earl Percy.
First Record: 1822 / Last Record: 1834

EDINBURGH CASTLE

26 Bell Street

The **Edinburgh Castle** stood towards the eastern end of Bell Street, at the foot of, and adjacent to Stewart's Bank Stairs. *First Record: 1855 / Last Record: 1865*

EDINBURGH CASTLE

80 Clive Street

Unusually, two public houses of this name existed in North Shields Low Town only a short distance from each other. Despite distinct addresses being evident, there is a high possibility that they may have been the same premises or mis-recorded.
First Record: 1822 / Last Record: 1834

ELEPHANT AND CASTLE

19 Camden Street

An unusual combination of names for a pub, with two theories: The *'Castle'* here is the howdah on the back of an elephant. Alternatively it may be a corruption of *'Infanta de Castile'*, usually said to be a reference to Eleanor of Castile, the wife of Edward I (in Spain and Portugal, the *'infanta'* was the eldest daughter of the monarch without a claim to the throne). *First Record: 1850 / Last Record: 1850*

EMPIRE

72 Tyne Street *First Record: 1897 / Last Record: 1912*

ENGLISH AND FRENCH FLAG

Bell Street / Bland Square

The reason for this unusual combination of names is unknown; however it is likely to have been derived from the Napoleonic Wars. The exact location of the premises is unconfirmed. *First Record: 1855 / Last Record: 1855*

ESLINGTON HOUSE

33 Camden Street

The first known reference to Eslington is in 1334 which referred to a stone tower in the civil parish of Whittingham, Northumberland. It has not been established why this public house should bear a related name. *First Record: 1834 / Last Record: 1834*

ESSEX ARMS

2 Duke Street / 23 Duke Street

The **Essex Arms** was situated at the south end of Duke Street, at the edge of the Bull Ring. *First Record: 1850 / Last Record: 1887*

EUROPEAN

Steels Quay *First Record: 1867 / Last Record: 1867*

EUROPEAN AND UNITED STATES

5 Railway Terrace / 11 Railway Terrace

The unusually named **European and United States** (or the **County Hotel***) as it was latterly known, stood opposite North Shields Railway Station, to the south side of Railway Terrace, between Rudyerd Street and Little Bedford Street.
First Record: 1865 / Last Record: 1968

European and United States, Railway Terrace, c.1920.

EXCHANGE HOTEL (Refer to: EXCHANGE VAULTS)
31 Clive Street / 51 Clive Street

EXCHANGE INN (Refer to: EXCHANGE VAULTS)
31 Clive Street / 51 Clive Street

EXCHANGE VAULTS
(Refer to: **WATERLOO INN**)
31 Clive Street / 51 Clive Street
Also referred to as the **Exchange Hotel** and the **Exchange Inn**.

EXPRESS INN
Nile Street
Only recorded in directories during 1938, this public house stood on the corner of Nile Street and Russell Street. *First Record: 1938 / Last Record: 1938*

FALCON ARMS
37 Dotwick Street
The pub name is likely to have been derived from the ancient sport of falconry. *First Record: 1865 / Last Record: 1865*

FERRY HOUSE
1 Duke Street / New Quay
There have been several derivations of the name of this public house,

The Exchange Hotel, Clive Street, c.1931.

which was generally and simply known as the 'Ferry', and it was one of the smallest public houses in North Shields. Originally called the **Steam Ferry House** or **Steam Packet**, and sometimes referred to as the **Steamboat**, it was shortened to the **Ferry House**, and was a small inn, which took its name from the Steam Ferry Station which stood only a few yards away on the river.

Situated on the east side of Duke Street, directly opposite the **Crane House Vaults** and the **Crown & Thistle**, it was separated by a narrow alleyway from the **Sussex Arms**. The inn stood next to Grindstone Stairs, an alleyway which ran from Duke Street and ending with a set of steps to the Riverside. *First Record: 1822 / Last Record: 1887*

FLAG
Bland's Square Quay
Early maps show the **Flag**, as overlooking the River Tyne on Blands Square Quay on part of the site also indicated as being occupied by the **Black Swan Inn**.
First Record: Unconfirmed / Last Record: Unconfirmed

FLINNS (Refer to: NORTH EASTERN HOTEL)
42 Nile Street / 17 West Percy Street
Originally referred to as the **Spirit of Dublin Porter Vaults**, these premises were renamed **Flinns**. The building was demolished in order to make way for the **North Eastern Hotel**. *First Record: 1847 / Last Record: 1897*

FLOWER POT
Albion Street / 14 Albion Road West
The **Flower Pot** existed until 1850, when, soon afterwards it was renamed as the **Spring Gardens Inn**. It was a well known landmark of its day, and was the first calling station in North Shields of the old stage coaches which is believed to have stood on this

site since about 1690. It was renowned as an 'open-air' public house, as many of the tables were arranged in the large flower garden at the rear of the inn, which also had a large pond stocked with goldfish and was a great attraction in bygone days.

The premises came into the possession of Newcastle Breweries and, in 1934, was rebuilt to its present format, with the frontage being very similar in style and design to that of the **Cannon** at Billy Mill, the **Collingwood Arms** at Chirton and the **Foxhunters** at Preston Gate. *First Record: 1822-50 as the Flower Pot / Last Record: 1850 – Extant 2013 as the Spring Gardens Inn.*

FOG ON THE TYNE (Refer to COLONEL LINSKILL)
Charlotte Street

FOUL ANCHOR (Refer to ANCHOR TAVERN)
Swans Quay / Clive Street / 14 Duke Street / 18 Duke Street

FOUNTAIN HEAD
91 Bedford Street
Built on the site of the **Old Phoenix Tavern**, the **Fountain Head** (*below, c.1960*) stood on the west side of Bedford Street, slightly to the north of its junction with Wellington Street. Until its demolition in the 1970s to make way for new shops, the **Fountain Head** was one of a small number of public houses in the area which retained the original glazed terracotta faience and original pub signage above the windows and entrance. *First Record: 1897 / Last Record: 1968*

FREE GARDNERS ARMS
57 Camden Street *First Record: 1886 / Last Record: 1905*

FREEMASONS ARMS
3 Bell Street
The **Freemasons Arms** was located on Lamb Quay, and overlooked the River Tyne, at the rear of Bell Street. The larger **Nags Head** adjoined this pub at the corner of Lamb Quay and Bell Street. *First Record: 1850 / Last Record: 1850*

FRIENDLY TAVERN
Church Row / 9 Church Way / 10 Church Way *First Record: 1822 / Last Record: 1865*

FUTURE ADMIRAL

Wellington Street
The reason for this unusual name has not been ascertained.
First Record: 1847 / Last Record: 1847

GARDNERS ARMS

50 Rudyerd Street / 1 Gardner Street
The **Gardners Arms** (*below, c.1961*) was named after Ralph Gardner a brewer of Chirton Green, who petitioned Oliver Cromwell's Parliament in 1655, about the restrictions on trade, placed by Newcastle. He wrote the petition from his prison cell and called it *'England's Grievances Discovered'*.
First Record: 1938 / Last Record: Late 1970s

GARIBALDI ARMS

37 Church Way
Guiseppe Garibaldi was an Italian nationalist and leader who visited Tynemouth in 1854. The public house was probably named after him after he led 1,000 volunteers in the capture of Sicily and Naples in 1860. His conquest led to the formation of the kingdom of Italy in 1861. *First Record: 1865 / Last Record: 1865*

GARRICKS HEAD

23 Saville Street / 25 Saville Street / 52 Saville Street
Situated on the south side of Saville Street, the **Garricks Head** was so named as a tribute to David Garrick, (1717-79), a British actor and theatre manager who was considered the foremost Shakespearean player of his time.

As one of North Shields' oldest public houses, it was originally a small building, with glazed brickwork and an adjacent covered alleyway, however in more recent years it was extended by alterations to the adjoining buildings, thereby enlarging the entire premises as far as the corner with Camden Street.

The original **Garricks Head** building is one of a small number of public houses in the area which has retained the original glazed terracotta faience as well as the original pub signage above the windows and entrance. Although the pub dates prior to 1822, an ornamental glazed scroll above the door incorporates a rebuilding date of 1899.
First Record: 1822 / Last Record: Extant 2013

GENERAL HAVELOCK

25 Saville Street / 38 Saville Street / 40 Saville Street / 42 Saville Street / 10 Camden Street

At one time, the **General Havelock** was one of the largest public houses in North Shields. The sheer size of the building, dominated a corner site to the south side of Saville Street, and the western side of Camden Street.

Named after Major General Sir Henry Havelock (1795-1857), a

The General Havelock, Saville Street / Camden Street, c.1962.

native of Bishopwearmouth, Sunderland, whose heroic successes during the Indian Mutiny of 1857 earned him considerable praise from military leaders, politicians and newspaper editors in Britain. He was hailed as an example of 'military excellence and devout character'. He became a popular hero, depicting all that was great about the British Empire in the mid 19th century. While his popularity grew in Britain, Havelock was still fighting in India and probably never realised the extent of his fame.

Similarly, Sir Colin Campbell was in command of troops during the Indian Mutiny at this time, and the public house situated at the west end of Saville Street bears his name.

Prior to demolition in the late 1990s, the **General Havelock** was renamed for a short time as 'O'Keefe's'. In 2007, it was replaced with a small supermarket.

First Record: 1865 / Last Record: 1990s

GEORGE TAVERN

68 King Street / 70 King Street / 73 King Street.

The **George Tavern** was generally known as the **Old George Tavern**, and was situated on the western side, close to the foot of King Street near the junction with Charlotte Street.

In 1800, when the streets of North Shields were badly maintained, and the neighbourhood above the bank top mostly consisted of fields, with only a few houses scattered here and there, there was one inn of which the folk of Shields were proud – the famous **George Tavern**, in King Street. This inn was one of great importance in the history of North Shields, as it contained a large assembly room, where the magistracy administered the law of the town from. It was the centre of function and authority. The room was brilliantly lit by a large crystal chandelier, and the tea and other rooms were spacious and comfortable. Dance clubs held at the premises were exclusive, and members were carefully selected before being proposed or admitted, and only the most aristocratic of the town were allowed to join. The magnificent balls that were held there were very elaborate affairs. Seated in the parlour, on ancient wheel-back armchairs, gigantic platefuls of English Roast Beef were partaken, the firelight mellowing the old coaching prints that hung around the room.

The commemoration of the jubilee of King George, on 25th October 1809, was celebrated in the town by the ringing of Christ Church bells, and in the evening by a grand ball and supper in the **George Tavern**. The proceeds of this ball, augmented by general subscriptions, were devoted to the building of the Royal Jubilee School, for the education of poor girls and boys.

In the 1860s Rev. John Broadbent, a Wesleyan minister and temperance reformer, arrived in the town and upon seeing the volume of drunkenness of the inhabitants, he worked with untiring energy until under his Christian influence, a great change was effected in North Shields, to better the people both morally and spiritually. It was this single advocate of temperance who is reputed to have eventually killed the popularity of the **George Tavern**. *First Record: 1822 / Last Record: 1940*

GEORGE IV

Clive Street / Applebys Bank
A very short-lived establishment, this was the first of two public houses recorded in North Shields by this name. *First Record: 1827 / Last Record: 1827*

GEORGE IV

91 Bell Street
The **George IV** Public House was located on the south side of Bell Street, adjacent to Maitland's Lane, which led to Maitland's Quay.

It was named after George IV, King of Great Britain and Ireland and of Hanover from 1820 to 1830, who caused controversy when he attempted to divorce his estranged wife, Caroline of Brunswick. The pub was renamed as the **Sailors Return** in 1855.
*First Record: 1833-55 as **George IV** / Last Record: 1855-61 as the **Sailors Return***

GLOBE

56 Bell Street
The first of two public houses recorded by this name in North Shields, the **Globe** stood towards the eastern end of Bell Street, near the foot of Fenwick's Bank Stairs.
First Record: 1822 / Last Record: 1855

GLOBE INN

20 Clive Street
The **Globe Inn** was situated on Clive Street, immediately next to the Hole in the Wall Quay to the south, and Bird in Hand Quay to the north. It was often referred to as the 'Marble Bar'. *First Record: 1855 / Last Record: 1887*

GOLDEN EAGLE

Union Street *First Record: 1822 / Last Record: 1827*

GOLDEN FLEECE

11 New Quay
Situated to the east side of Clive Street, at the foot of Borough Road (Bank) junction, the **Golden Fleece** is the most southerly of all the inns and taverns on Clive Street, with the front of the building facing Duke Street and the New Quay.

A **Golden Fleece** has stood on this site since the early-mid 1800s, and the present structure, rebuilt in 1897, stood just a few feet away from the **Old Black Lion** and the **Percy Arms**, to the rear on Steam Mill Lane and Clive Street. The first **Golden Fleece** was only half the size of the present structure, and was approximately 60 years old when it was demolished to make way for the existing building, which was designed by W&T.R. Milburn of Sunderland.

The unusual architecture consists of a central first floor arched balcony, which is dominated on each side with two ornate gables, each of which are topped with a sandstone finial. A decorative oriel multipaned window and a semicircular arched multipaned window adorn the ground floor of the premises, which has remained unchanged since it was built. Originally, the pub had a long single counter which served an 'L' shaped bar and other small sitting rooms.

Right: Plan of the Golden Fleece, c.1897.

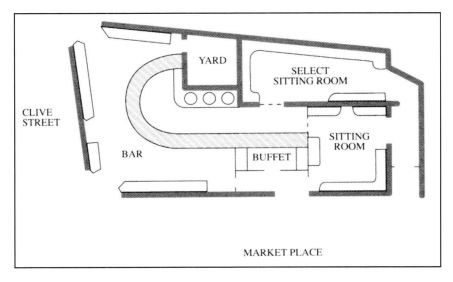

The Golden Fleece, New Quay, c.1956.

Modernisation over recent years, has meant that much of the original interior splendour has been lost with lowered ceilings, rooms opened out and a background theme based on the interior of a ship, hence the change of name in the mid 1980s to the **Porthole**. At the end of the 19th century, there were more than 100 public houses along the length of North Shields riverside, and this is one of the last remaining ones. In 2004, the building was considered to be one of special architectural or historic interest, and was recorded with Grade 2 listed building status.
*First Record: 1834 – c.1984 as the **Golden Fleece** /*
*Last Record: c.1984 – Extant 2013 as the **Porthole**.*

GOLDEN FLEECE

71 Norfolk Street / 72 Norfolk Street
North Shields had two public houses with the unusual name of the Golden Fleece, the name being taken from the winged ram in the legend of Jason and the Argonauts in Greek mythology.

The **Golden Fleece** adjoined the side of St. Columba's United Reformed Church Hall, fronting Northumberland Square. The **Golden Fleece** itself was located on the west side of Norfolk Street and was later converted to a house, with an adjacent covered alleyway. *First Record: 1865 / Last Record: 1920*

The Golden Fleece (converted to a house), Norfolk Street, c.2013.

GOLDEN LION INN

12 Union Street / 35 Union Street / 36 Union Street / Church Way
Originally standing on the east side of Church Way, the **Golden Lion** was extended in the later part of the 1800s to incorporate the building on the northern corner of Union Street to become a corner site. The inn stood directly opposite the **Prince of Wales**, near to the top of Causey Bank. *First Record: 1822 / Last Record: 1928*

GOLDEN LION

Clive Street

The second of two public houses recorded in North Shields by this name during the same year. The name was probably adopted from English heraldry in which a golden lion is often depicted. *First Record: 1822 / Last Record: 1834*

GREENLAND FISHERY

Charlotte Street

Presumably so named because of the local connection with the fishing trade. *First Record: 1822 / Last Record: 1834*

GREEN MAN

14 Liddell Street / 15 Liddell Street / 22 Liddell Street / Pandon Bank

The unusually named **Green Man** was a large building which stood at the commencement of the narrowest part of Liddell Street, adjacent to the steep stairs of Green Man Bank, (Pandon Bank Stairs). It was situated on the north side of the road directly opposite the **Crown and Cushion**, the **Dock Hotel** and the **Trawlers Arms**. The original images of a Green Man are often found in churches as a face peering through leaves and petals; this character is the Will o' the Wisp. Some pub signs will also show a Green Man as he appears in English traditional sword dances (in green tats). The Green Man may also be linked to the legend of Robin Hood. The **Green Man** was later renamed the **Black Bull Inn**.

First Record: 1822 as the Green Man / Last Record: 1899 as the Black Bull Inn

GREY HORSE (Refer to: GRIDIRON HOUSE)

55 Bell Street / Grey Horse Quay

GREY HORSE

Bull Ring

The second public house listed under this name in North Shields. *First Record: 1822 / Last Record: 1834*

GREYHOUND

Bird Street / Beacon Street / Toll Street

The first public house listed under this name in North Shields. *First Record: 1822 / Last Record: 1851*

GREYHOUND

Bell Street

The second public house listed under this name in North Shields. *First Record: 1834 / Last Record: 1834*

GREYHOUND

22 Church Street / 25 Church Street

The third public house listed under this name in North Shields. *First Record: 1834 / Last Record: 1855*

GRIDIRON HOUSE

55 Bell Street

There is no known significance to the original name of this public house which in 1850 was renamed as the **Low Grey Horse** but was known as just the **Grey Horse**. *First Record: 1847 as the Gridiron House / Last Record: 1855 as the Grey Horse*

HALF MOON INN

Low Lights / Back Union Road

The **Half Moon Inn** was one of the many buildings forming the area around the Low Lights. It was located to the east of, and behind Union Road near to Cliffords Fort. The neighbouring **Waggon Inn** stood on Union Road, slightly offset to the rear of the **Half Moon Inn**. *First Record: 1822 / Last Record: 1940*

HARE AND HOUNDS
Collingwood Street *First Record: 1847 / Last Record: 1847*

HARTLEY HOUSE
Shepherds Quay *First Record: 1834 / Last Record: 1834*

HIBERNIAN TAVERN
Bell Street
'Hibernia' is the Latin and poetic name for the island of Ireland, so there may well have been an Irish connection when this pub was so named. The exact location is unconfirmed. *First Record: 1855 / Last Record: 1855*

HIGHLANDER HOTEL
41 Liddell Street / Union Road / Union Quay
Sometimes referred to as the **Old Highlander**, this pub was rebuilt on the site of an earlier pub of the same name. The **Highlander** (*below, c.1920*) was a large inn which faced the River Tyne on the north side of Union Quay. The building stood close to the **Newcastle Arms** and the **Lord Collingwood**, and slightly to the east of the foot of Naters Bank Stairs. The actual building was converted to a grocer's shop which became popularly known as William Wight's Store. *First Record: 1834 / Last Record: 1930*

HOPE INN
41 Norfolk Street
The **Hope Inn** was situated on the east side of Norfolk Street. It was situated close to the old fire station which later became the **Bell and Bucket**.
First Record: 1855 / Last Record: 1940

HOPE AND ANCHOR
Low Lights / Back Union Road
The **Hope and Anchor** was a very small inn, and stood on that part of the area known as the Low Lights. It was situated to the east of, and behind Union Road near Cliffords Fort. The neighbouring **Queens Head** stood directly next door to it.
First Record: 1822 / Last Record: 1855

HOPE AND ANCHOR

16 Bell Street / 28 Bell Street

The **Hope and Anchor** was the second public house in North Shields to bear this name. It stood on the north side of Bell Street, at the foot of Turpin's Bank Stairs.
First Record: 1822 / Last Record: 1887

HOPE AND ANCHOR

Duke Street

The third public house in North Shields to bear this name, which is in fact a common name for many public houses situated throughout the country. The name takes its origin from the Bible, Hebrews 6:19: *"We have this as a sure and steadfast anchor of the soul, a hope".* Exact location unconfirmed. *First Record: 1822 / Last Record: 1827*

HOWICK HALL

9 Bedford Street

This public house was named after Howick Hall, the home of the Grey family from 1319. The best known member of the family was the 2nd Earl Grey, who was Prime Minister responsible for passing the Great Reform Bill of 1832 and whose monument stands at the top of Grey Street in Newcastle. *First Record: 1834 / Last Record: 1834*

HYLTON CASTLE

28 Dotwick Street

The **Hylton Castle** stood directly next door to the **Vulcans Arms** public house on the west side of Dotwick Street. Although there is no obvious connection to North Shields, it is reasonable to assume that this public house was named after Hylton Castle near Sunderland which was built by Sir William Hylton as his principal residence in about 1400.

An Ordnance Survey map dated 1886 indicates that these buildings were superseded by the **Clarendon Hotel**. *First Record: 1850 / Last Record: 1855*

IMPERIAL ARMS

19 Church Street *First Record: 1887 / Last Record: 1887*

INDUSTRY

Coble Dene Bank

Although listed in an 1855 directory, as simply the **Industry**, the premises were known as both the **Lodge of Industry** and the **Cottage of Industry**.

The building overlooked the River Tyne to the south side of Coble Dene Bank. Bearing in mind that during the 1800s, Coble Dene incorporated a lot of heavy shipping industry, the name for the pub was probably relative to the busy riverside trades. *First Record: 1850 / Last Record: 1855*

JERUSALEM COFFEE HOUSE

Clive Street

Situated to the east side of Clive Street, the unusually named **Jerusalem Coffee House** was tucked away overlooking the river, behind the **Kings Head** public house, on the Jerusalem Coffee House Quay. The origins of this name were likely to have been derived from similarly named old coffee houses of London which were popular during the late 17th and early 18th centuries. *First Record: 1822 / Last Record: 1855*

JOHN BULL INN

135 Church Street

Also known as the **John Bull Tavern**, this was one of the smaller inns of the High Town, and stood on the west side of Church Street, not far from the junction with Lower Pearson Street (later to become Charlotte Street).

John Bull was a caricature created by Dr John Arbuthnot in 1712 and was usually depicted as a stout, middle-aged, jolly man who became a national personification of Great Britain. The character was often used in political cartoons and similar graphic works. *First Record: 1834 / Last Record: 1920*

JOHN BULL TAVERN (Refer to: **JOHN BULL INN**)
135 Church Street

JOLLY SAILOR
Clive Street / Bird-in-Hand Quay *First Record: 1850 / Last Record: 1850*

KEEL AND FIDDLE
41 Dotwick Street / Dock Lane
The unusual name of this pub probably originates from the freight barges that were used for carrying coal on the River Tyne, along with the violins or 'fiddles' that the keelmen would sometimes play. *First Record: 1822 / Last Record: 1834*

KINGS ARMS
62 Clive Street
The **Kings Arms** is a common name for pubs both in England and elsewhere. The name refers to the coat of arms of a king, which a pub of this name would display prominently above its door as a means of identifying it.
First Record: 1822 / Last Record: 1850

KINGS ARMS
Duke Street
This was the second public house recorded with this name in North Shields.
First Record: 1822 / Last Record: 1834

KINGS HEAD
Clive Street / Jerusalem Coffee House Quay
This was the first of six public houses recorded with this name in North Shields and was situated to the east side of Clive Street. The **Kings Head** adjoined the **Jerusalem Coffee House**, on the Jerusalem Coffee House Quay.
First Record: 1822 / Last Record: 1887

KINGS HEAD
Union Street
This was the second of six public houses recorded with this name in North Shields.
First Record: 1822 / Last Record: 1822

KINGS HEAD
Walker Place
This was the third of six public houses recorded with this name in North Shields.
First Record: 1827 / Last Record: 1827

KINGS HEAD
103 Hudson Street
The **Kings Head** was originally a fairly small pub, standing on the high bank top, overlooking the Fish Quay from the foot of Hudson Street, near the junction with Tyne Street. Over the years, alteration work was carried out to extend the building to its present format, and during the 1990s it became another victim of change, when as an ailing pub, the name was changed to the **Wooden Doll** in an effort to revive its popularity. Over recent years it has supported live music, and has been a favourite venue for musicians, groups and families. This was the fourth of six public houses recorded with this name in North Shields. *First Record: 1827 / Last Record: 2007*

KINGS HEAD
34 Duke Street
This was the fifth of six public houses recorded with this name in North Shields.
First Record: 1834 / Last Record: 1834

KINGS HEAD
162 Church Street / 163 Church Street
This was the sixth and last public house recorded with this name in North Shields. The **Kings Head** stood on the west side of Church Street, a short distance north of the junction with Tyne Street. *First Record: 1834 / Last Record: 1912*

KING WILLIAM IV
Brunswick Place / Coble Dene
The **King William IV** stood close to the River Tyne on the north side of Brunswick Place, near the junction with West Row. Named after William IV, who was King of Great Britain and Ireland (1830-37), and ascended to the throne after a long naval career. Leaving no direct heir, he was succeeded by his niece Victoria. *First Record: 1834 / Last Record: 1855*

KING WILLIAM IV
28 Hudson Street
This was the second of two public houses recorded under this name in North Shields. Named in honour of William IV (1830-37), this public house was located near the junction with Bird Street, and was a fairly insignificant building which stood on the west side of Hudson Street, backing onto James Square. *First Record: 1850 / Last Record: 1855*

KIRKCALDY ARMS
(Refer to: **OLD LIGHTHOUSE**)
35 Bell Street
Presumably named after the town of Kirkcaldy in the Royal Burgh of Fife, there is no known obvious connection with the name to North Shields. *First Record: 1822 / Last Record: 1887-1907 as the **Kirkcaldy Arms***

Right: The Kirkcaldy Arms, Bell Street, c.1900.

LAMB
21 Bell Street / 23 Bell Street / Bland Square
This name could well have been adopted from religious symbolism, taken from John 1:29: *"Behold the Lamb of God, which taketh away the sins of the world".* *First Record: 1822 / Last Record: 1850*

LAMB INN
16 Dotwick Street / 17 Dotwick Street
The **Lamb** was a small Public House situated between the **Bee Hive** and the **Vulcans Arms** on the west side of Dotwick Street. *First Record: 1822 / Last Record: 1855*

LAMBTON CASTLE

1 Wellington Street /
2 Wellington Street
The **Lambton Castle** was a lock-up establishment, with no residential accommodation, which stood on the north-east corner of Wellington Street at its junction with Little Bedford Street. It appears that the name was derived from the stately home of the same name, situated in Co. Durham.
First Record: 1897 /
Last Record: 1981

The Lambton Castle, Wellington Street, c.1963.

LANGLEY CASTLE

16 Cobourg Terrace / 16 Cobourg Street
The **Langley Castle** stood on the north side of Tynemouth Road (Coburg Terrace) just a few yards west of the **Coburg Hotel**, and directly opposite the top of Hudson Street. The inn, which has since been converted to residential flats, is now numbered 102 and 104 Tynemouth Road.
First Record: 1865 / Last Record: 1930

Left: The Langley Castle (converted to a house), Coburg Terrace, c.2010.

LAUREL ARMS

(Refer to: **COLONEL LINSKILL**)
Charlotte Street

LETTERS

Bull Ring
An unusually named establishment with an unknown origin.
First Record: 1822 / Last Record: 1822

LASS O'GOWRIE

Clive Street
The '*Lass O'Gowrie*' was a poem written by Lady Carolina Nairne (1766-1845), a Scottish poet who was well known during her lifetime. Most of her work was published under a pseudonym. Gowrie is an area of farm belt famous for its fruit, in Perth and Kinross, central Scotland, along the northern shore of the Firth of Tay, between Perth and Dundee. The pub was no doubt named in tribute to the poem.
First Record: 1850 / Last Record: 1850

LINDSAY ARMS

25 Clive Street / 26 Clive Street
The **Lindsay Arms** stood on the east side of Clive Street, separated from the **Star and Garter** inn beside the alleyway leading to Steel's Quay. To the rear of the **Lindsay Arms**, the lesser known **Dutalia Hotel** adjoined it and backed onto the River Tyne.
First Record: 1865 / Last Record: 1887

LINSKILL ARMS

1 Grey Street

The **Linskill Arms** was situated on the corner of Grey Street and North Church Street. The origins of the name stem from the prominent Linskill family who were once major landowners in North Shields. *First Record: 1865 / Last Record: 1865*

LODGE OF INDUSTRY (Refer to: INDUSTRY)

Coble Dene Bank

LOMBARD ARMS

15 Clive Street / Lishmans Quay

The **Lombard Arms** stood on the east side of Clive Street, opposite the foot of Barnes Bank, next to Lishmans Quay. Lombard is a word that relates to a Germanic tribe that dominated northern Italy and adjoining areas from the 6th to 8th centuries, and there is no obvious connection to North Shields. *First Record: 1855 / Last Record: 1887*

LONDONDERRY ARMS

Clive Street

The **Londonderry Arms** stood on the west side of Clive Street opposite the **Star & Garter Inn**. Wascoe's Bank Stairs separated it from the **Board Inn** which stood next door. Possibly named because of Irish connections in the town.
First Record: 1855 / Last Record: 1855

LORD BROUGHAM

21 Middle Street

The **Lord Brougham** stood on the west side of Middle Street, at the corner with Raff Yard, which was a lane connecting North Street and Middle Street.

The pub was named after Henry Brougham who was born in Edinburgh on 19th September 1778. He developed a reputation as a lawyer which brought him to the attention of the leaders of the Whigs. Brougham was given the task of organising the Whigs press campaign in the 1807 General Election and in 1810 he accepted a parliamentary seat in order to enter the House of Commons. Brougham soon established himself as one of the leading radicals in Parliament, and in the House of Commons he became the leading spokesmen for the radicals. In 1830 Brougham was given a peerage and became Lord Chancellor in Lord Grey's new Whig government. Brougham, who had been arguing for parliamentary reform for over thirty years, played an important role in persuading the House of Lords to pass the 1832 Reform Act. Lord Brougham was also one of the main people behind the passing of the 1833 Anti-Slavery Act. He died on 17th May 1868. *First Record: 1834 / Last Record: 1855*

LORD BROUGHAM

Church Street

This was the second public house recorded with this name in North Shields.
First Record: 1834 / Last Record: 1834

LORD BYRON

17 Stephenson Street / 24 Stephenson Street

Named after Lord George Byron, the famous Anglo-Scottish Poet (1788-1824) and situated diagonally opposite the **Crown and Sceptre** public house, the **Lord Byron** public house stood on the east side of Stephenson Street, not far from the junction with Saville Street/Charlotte Street. *First Record: 1834 / Last Record: 1920*

LORD COLLINGWOOD

10 Union Quay / Union Row / Union Road

The **Lord Collingwood** stood at the foot of Naters Bank Stairs, and faced the River Tyne on the north side of Union Quay. The building was situated directly next door to the **Newcastle Arms**, the site of which later became the Fishermen's Mission, and was undoubtedly named after Lord Cuthbert Collingwood.
First Record: 1822 / Last Record: 1930

The Newcastle Arms and the Lord Collingwood, Union Quay, c.1896.

LORD CORNWALLIS
Clive Street
This public house was probably named in honour of Charles Cornwallis, First Marquis and Second Earl Cornwallis (1738-1805). He was a British military and political leader who commanded forces in North Carolina during the American Revolution. His surrender at Yorktown in 1781 marked the final British defeat.
First Record: 1822 / Last Record: 1827

LORD DELAVAL
51 Church Street *First Record: 1847 / Last Record: 1847*

LORD HOWARTH
Toll Street
No references can be found to ascertain why this public house was so named, or who Lord Howarth was during the time this building existed.
First Record: 1834 / Last Record: 1834

LORD JOHN RUSSELL
61 Camden Street
This public house was named after John Russell, (First Earl Russell 1792-1878), a British politician who served as prime minister from 1846-52 & 1865-66, and advocated parliamentary reform. *First Record: 1834 / Last Record: 1834*

LORD NELSON (Refer to: ADMIRAL NELSON)
69 George Street

LORD NELSON
Toll Street *First Record: 1847 / Last Record: 1852*

LORD NELSON (Refer to: ADMIRAL NELSON)
29 Liddell Street / 49 Liddell Street

LORD NELSON
31 Camden Street / 32 Camden Street / 63 Camden Street
Named after Admiral Lord Horatio Nelson, the greatest hero in British naval history, this public house was a fairly small and innocuous building which stood on the east side of Camden Street near the junction with Saville Street. Eventually demolished, the site is now occupied by part of the multi storey car park and service area of North Shields Shopping Mall. *First Record: 1834 / Last Record: 1968*

LOW GREY HORSE (Refer to: GRIDIRON HOUSE)
55 Bell Street / Grey Horse Quay

LOW LIGHTS TAVERN
8 Brewhouse Bank / Low Lights
Although first recorded in 1834, the **Low Lights** (*below, c.1985*) is believed to have been an ale house since the 16th century and is situated on the east side of Brewhouse Bank not far from the Low Lights area. It is the oldest surviving tavern still standing in the former 'Low Town' of North Shields, and retains a typical charm and 'Olde Worlde' character that it probably possessed when it was first built. In the 1800s the Low Lights Brewery and Maltings formed the adjoining buildings, hence the name of Brewhouse or Brewery Bank. *First Record: 1834 / Last Record: Extant 2013*

LOYAL STANDARD
Bell Street *First Record: 1822 / Last Record: 1834*

LUCKY BOB
Clive Street
The origins of the name remain a mystery. Nothing is known of who or what *'Lucky Bob'* was. *First Record: 1851 / Last Record: 1851*

LUMPERS ARMS
15 Clive Street / Lishmans Quay
The **Lumpers Arms** stood towards the east side of Clive Street, adjacent to Lishmans Quay, and overlooked the river to the rear. A *'Lumper'* was a term for a stevedore or dock worker. By 1896, the pub was replaced by the **Lombard Arms**, situated next door on Clive Street. *First Record: 1855 / Last Record: 1887*

MAGNESIA BANK
1 Camden Street
The **Magnesia Bank** is a relatively new public house, which opened in 1989, prior to which it had been better known as North Shields Central Club. Originally constructed as a Commerce Bank in the 1800s, and situated on the west side of Camden Street at the junction with Union Street, the building stood close to the nearby steps leading from Union Street to the Low Town, which were known as Magnesia Bank Stairs, which loaned their name to the pub. *First Record: 1989 / Last Record: Extant 2013*

MAGPIE
Coble Dene *First Record: 1850 / Last Record: 1855*

MARINERS ARMS
1 Saville Street West
Although the **Mariners Arms** was one of the older public houses in North Shields, the first directory listing did not appear until 1938. Situated opposite the **Ballarat Hotel**, it stands on the north east corner of Saville Street West and Borough Road. For many years, the **Mariners Arms** was simply an ale house, as there was no licence to retail wines or spirits of any kind, however an application was made in the 1970s to change this, and the appropriate spirit licence was subsequently granted. In 1991, the name of the pub was changed to the **Betty Baddoo**, as a tribute to a landlady there, however this proved to be a very unpopular choice, and less than a year later, the name reverted back to its former and traditional name; the **Mariners Arms**.
First Record: 1938 / Last Record: Extant 2013

MARINERS ARMS
Church Street *First Record: 1850 / Last Record: 1850*

MARINERS ARMS
28 Bell Street *First Record: 1834 / Last Record: 1834*

MARQUIS OF GRANBY
1 Church Street / 31 Tyne Street
The **Marquis of Granby** was a corner inn, situated on the east side of Church Street at its junction with Tyne Street, and was always locally referred to simply as *'The Granby'*. The Marquis of Granby, John Manners, was a general in the 18th century who showed a great concern for the welfare of his men upon their retirement and provided funds for many to establish taverns, which were subsequently named after him.
First Record: 1822 / Last Record: 1940

MARQUIS OF LORNE
Tynemouth Road / 15 Pearson Terrace / 16 Pearson Terrace / Upper Queen Street
The **Marquis of Lorne** formerly occupied a site on the south side of Tynemouth Road, at its junction on the west side of Upper Queen Street. The pub derived its name from John Sutherland Campbell, 9th Duke of Argyll (1845-1914) who was better known by the courtesy title of the Marquess of Lorne and was the fourth Governor-General of Canada from 1878 to 1883. *First Record: 1887 / Last Record: 1968*

MASH TUN (Refer to COBOURG HOTEL)
Coburg Street / Tynemouth Road

MASONIC ARMS
70 Bedford Street / 71 Bedford Street
The **Masonic Arms**, or **Masons Arms** as it was sometimes known, was situated on the west side of Bedford Street, a few yards south of its junction with West Percy Street. It is not known if the pub had any significant connection with Freemasonry as the name suggests. *First Record: 1865 / Last Record: 1928*

MASONS ARMS (Refer to MASONIC ARMS)
70 Bedford Street / 71 Bedford Street

MASONS ARMS
64 Stephenson Street / 161 Stephenson Street
The **Masons Arms** stood on the west side of Stephenson Street about halfway between Upper Pearson Street and Charlotte Street, on the site of what became the telephone exchange. *First Record: 1850 / Last Record: 1940*

MASONS ARMS
Ropery Bank
As well as the Freemasons symbol of the Square and Compass inscribed within three circles, the **Masons Arms** also bore upon its sign the words; **Ship in Launch**, a name

by which the pub was also known. Why this particular sign was there, or what the words meant, no one knew. Had it been the 'Ship Inn Launch' or the 'Ship Launch Inn', the meaning might have been easier to understand, however the name **Ship in Launch** still remains a mystery. The premises were small, almost hidden from sight behind a number of buildings situated near to the foot of Tanners Bank, between Union Road and the River Tyne. *First Record: 1822 / Last Record: 1899*

METERS ARMS
Queen Street
The unusually named **Meters Arms** was located on the east side of Queen Street, between Upper Pearson Street and Charlotte Street.
First Record: 1855 / Last Record: 1855

NAGS HEAD
98 Bell Street
The **Nags Head** stood on the south side of Bell Street, at the corner with Lamb Quay to the east. Adjoining the pub to the rear was the **Freemasons Arms** which overlooked the River Tyne. *First Record: 1855 / Last Record: 1865*

NAVAL RESERVE
11 Bell Street *First Record: 1887 / Last Record: 1887*

NAVIGATION TAVERN
62 Stephenson Street *First Record: 1834 / Last Record: 1834*

NEPTUNE
Clive Street *First Record: 1850 / Last Record: 1850*

NEPTUNE TAVERN
Tyne Street *First Record: 1834 / Last Record: 1834*

NEVILLE HOTEL
Railway Terrace /
82 Rudyerd Street
The **Neville Hotel** stood on the west side of Rudyerd Street, at its junction with Railway Terrace. In September 2010 it ceased trading as a public house and by 2012 the building had been converted into flats. *First Record: 1865 / Last Record: c.2008*

Right: The Neville Hotel, Railway Terrace / Rudyerd Street, c.1964.

NEW BULL RING (Refer to: BULL RING INN)
3 Bull Ring / 10 Bull Ring

NEWCASTLE INN
Bedford Street
Situated on the west side of Bedford Street, opposite the **Waterloo Tavern**, the **Newcastle Inn** stood slightly to the south of the junction with West Percy Street.
First Record: Unconfirmed / Last Record: Unconfirmed

NEW CLARENDON
Appleby Street *First Record: 1910 / Last Record: 1997*

NEW DOCK INN (Refer to: DOCK INN)
60 North Street

NEW DOLPHIN INN
(Refer to: STAITH HOUSE)
57 Low Lights / Union Road
The name 'staith' is taken from a wooden structure which is fixed to the river bed to provide a mooring post for ships.

NEWCASTLE ARMS
10 Clive Street
Situated about 100 yards from the corner of Borough Road Bank, the **Newcastle Arms** stood on the west side of Clive Street opposite the entrance to Elders Quay.
First Record: 1822 /
Last Record: 1855

NEWCASTLE ARMS
11 Union Quay / Low Lights
The **Newcastle Arms** faced the River Tyne on the north side of Union Quay. The building was situated directly next door to the

The New Dock Inn, North Street, c.1929.

Lord Collingwood. The site of this inn was later replaced by the Fishermans Mission which in turn was converted to a restaurant. *First Record: 1822 / Last Record: 1930*

NEW PHOENIX (Refer to: PHOENIX TAVERN)
55 Bedford Street / 68 Bedford Street / 70 Bedford Street / 91 Bedford Street / 111 Bedford Street

NORFOLK ARMS
77 Norfolk Street
The **Norfolk Arms** was situated near to Northumberland Square, on the west side of Norfolk Street, beside the United Presbyterian Church.
First Record: 1855 / Last Record: 1855

NORTH EASTERN HOTEL
17 West Percy Street / 30 West Percy Street
Built on the site of an earlier public house called the **Spirit of Dublin Porter Vaults** and **Flinns**, the **North Eastern Hotel** occupied a corner site on the north side of West Percy Road at the junction with Nile Street. The premises were later converted to become a shop. *First Record: 1897 / Last Record: 1968*

NORTH STAR (Refer to: OLD LIGHTHOUSE)
35 Bell Street / 36 Bell Street

NORTHUMBERLAND ARMS
Little Bedford Street
The **Northumberland Arms** was a small single storey pub, situated on the east side of Little Bedford Street, and was locally referred to as '*The Dead House*'.
First Record: 1928 / Last Record: 1940

NORTHUMBERLAND ARMS HOTEL

10 New Quay / Market Place

Probably the most famous and widely known of all the licensed premises in North Shields, the **Northumberland Arms Hotel** stood on the New Quay, facing the old market place and River Tyne. Originally constructed as a four storey Town House for the Duke of Northumberland, the foundation stone of the building which became part of North Shields Market Place was laid on 14th October 1806. This fine building had two imposing stone pillars at the entrance, above which was the coat of arms of the Duke of Northumberland.

First sold in 1821, and by 1897, the entire building had been refurbished and redecorated, with the ground floor being redesigned to incorporate new service areas, consisting of a bar, buffet, select room and a dining room. The upper floors contained a large dining room, billiard room, coffee room, and smoke rooms, specifically to cater for the shipbuilding trade, with public functions, luncheons and dinners.

By 1903, the premises were sold to a Newcastle wine & spirit merchants of A.H. Higginbottom & Co, who controlled the premises until the 1920s. The Grade II listed building for many years, was better known by the nickname of 'The Jungle', which had an international reputation as a magnet for the thousands of hard-living mariners who came ashore here for entertainment. It is open to speculation as to why it was nicknamed 'The Jungle'; however the most probable explanation is because of the numerous exotic animal heads and trophies which once adorned the many rooms whilst in possession of the Duke. In 1989, the premises closed, and were converted to luxury flats. *First Record: 1822 / Last Record: 1989*

The Northumberland Arms Hotel, New Quay, c.1906.

NORTHUMBERLAND HOTEL

29 Bedford Street / 113 Bedford Street / Little Bedford Street

The **Northumberland Hotel** was situated between Bedford Street and Little Bedford Street, having an entrance on both streets. It was located on the west side of Bedford Street, about halfway between the Tiger Stairs and Saville Street.
First Record: 1822 / Last Record: 1940

NORTHUMBERLAND INN

Clive Street *First Record: 1851 / Last Record: 1851*

OAK TAVERN
32 Charlotte Street
The **Oak Tavern** was a small building which was situated on the south side of Charlotte Street, near to the junction with Beacon Street. It virtually backed on to the nearby **Brewers Arms** which stood on nearby Beacon Street.
First Record: 1850 / Last Record: 1865

ODDFELLOWS ARMS
56 Grey Street
This pub may have been named after its use as a meeting place by the Independent Order of Odd Fellows; a fraternal organisation derived from the English Oddfellows Lodges of the mid-1700s. *First Record: 1938 / Last Record: 1969*

ODDFELLOWS ARMS
Albion Road
The name of the **Oddfellows Arms** on Albion Road was taken from the original **Oddfellows Arms** which once stood nearby on Grey Street. Originally built as a house during the 1800s, and eventually falling into a state of dereliction, this is a relatively new pub which opened in 1986. It occupies part of the building which, during the 1960s up to the 1980s was remembered by many people as the 'Karlson Club' and 'Marlows'. *First Record: 1986 / Last Record: Extant 2013*

OLD BLACK LION (Refer to: BLACK LION)
5 Clive Street / 38 Clive Street / 40 Clive Street / Steam Mill Lane

OLD GEORGE TAVERN
(Refer to: **GEORGE TAVERN**)
68 King Street / 70 King Street / 73 King Street

OLD HIGHLANDER
69 Church Way
First Record: 1886 / Last Record: 1887

OLD HIGHLANDER
(Refer to: **HIGHLANDER**)
41 Liddell Street / Union Road / Union Quay

OLD INN
51 Nile Street
First Record: 1865 / Last Record: 1865

The Old George Tavern, King Street, c.1941.

OLD LIGHTHOUSE
35 Bell Street / 36 Bell Street
This building probably dates back to Elizabethan days, and as the name suggests, the **Old Lighthouse** most likely derived its name from the High Lighthouse which stood on Tyne Street, at the top of the bank above Bell Street. It later became the **North Star**, then the **Kirkcaldy Arms** before closure as a pub in 1907, when it became a butchers shop and then a grocers. It has been long since demolished.
*First Record: 1822-55 as the **Old Lighthouse** /*
*Second Record: 1855-87 as the **North Star** /*
*Last Record: 1887-1907 as the **Kirkcaldy Arms***

OLD PHOENIX TAVERN (Refer to: PHOENIX TAVERN)
55 Bedford Street / 68 Bedford Street / 70 Bedford Street / 91 Bedford Street / 111 Bedford Street

OLD POST OFFICE INN
20 Tyne Street / 65 Tyne Street / Post Office Stairs
The **Old Post Office Inn** was set slightly back from the road on the bank side of Tyne Street, where it accommodated the long set of 97 steps known as the Post Office Stairs which dropped down to Bell Street in the Low Town.
First Record: 1850 / Last Record: 1899

OLD RED LION INN (Refer to: RED LION INN)
Church Road / 37 Church Way / 103 Church Way / 104 Church Way / 105 Church Way / 27 Wellington Street

OLD SHAKESPEARE TAVERN (Refer to: SHAKESPEARE INN)
17 Clive Street / 31 Clive Street / 33 Clive Street / Shepherds Quay

ORDNANCE ARMS
Low Lights
As this building stood in the area known as the Low Lights, close to Cliffords Fort, it is probable that the early military connection of the fort loaned its name to the pub.
First Record: 1822 / Last Record: 1827

PACK HORSE
Clive Street *First Record: 1850 / Last Record: 1850*

PERCY ARMS
Clive Street / Steam Mill Lane
Situated opposite Britannia Bank Stairs, to the east side of Clive Street, the **Percy Arms** adjoined the **Old Black Lion**, which stood at the corner of Steam Mill Lane, and Clive Street behind the **Golden Fleece**. The building has long since been demolished and the site was later occupied by the North Eastern Rubber Company.
First Record: 1850 / Last Record: 1855

PERCY ARMS
24 West Percy Street / 38 West Percy Street / 50 West Percy Street
The **Percy Arms** was situated on the north side of West Percy Street between Nelson Street and Sidney Street. *First Record: 1855 / Last Record: 1930*

PERCY ARMS
Whitehill Point
This was a large building, situated next to the loading staithes at Whitehill Point, just a few yards away from the edge of the River Tyne. *First Record: 1850 / Last Record: 1855*

PERCY MAIN (OLD PERCY MAIN / PERCY MAIN COLLIERY)
28 Dotwick Street *First Record: 1822 / Last Record: 1834*

PERSIMMON ARMS
4 Nile Street
A persimmon is the edible fruit of a number of species of trees from which this public house takes its name. *First Record: 1869 / Last Record: 1932*

PHOENIX
Clive Street *First Record: 1822 / Last Record: 1834*

PHOENIX HOTEL (Refer to: PHOENIX INN)
32 Duke Street / 41 Duke Street / 42 Duke Street, / Union Court

PHOENIX HOTEL (Refer to: PHOENIX TAVERN)
55 Bedford Street / 68 Bedford Street / 70 Bedford Street / 91 Bedford Street /
111 Bedford Street

PHOENIX INN
32 Duke Street / 41 Duke Street / 42 Duke Street / Union Court
Situated directly opposite the **Sussex Arms**, the **Phoenix Inn**, also known as the
Phoenix Hotel stood between Kirby's Bank and Union Court, on the west side of Duke
Street, just a little to the south of the **Crane House Vaults** and the **Crown & Thistle**.
The pub dates back to at least 1850, and was rebuilt in 1902 for Newcastle Breweries.

   The original idea was to include a long full width bar to the front of the site, with a
select room and a sitting room to the rear, served by hatches from the bar counter.
The plans, however, were modified to make an 'L' shaped bar and the inclusion of a
shop, so as to earn a rental for the brewery. *First Record: 1822 / Last Record: 1955*

PHOENIX TAVERN
55 Bedford Street / 68 Bedford Street / 70 Bedford Street / 91 Bedford Street /
111 Bedford Street
The **Phoenix Tavern** was also known by a variety of names, including the **Old Phoenix
Tavern**, the **Phoenix Hotel**, and also the **New Phoenix**. Situated on the west side of
Bedford Street, it stood a little to the north of its junction with Wellington Street, and in
1887 was better known as the **Bedford Hotel**. After demolition, the **Fountain Head** was
built on the same site.
*First Record: 1822 as the **Phoenix Tavern** / Last Record: 1887 as the **Bedford Hotel***

PINEAPPLE
52 King Street / 53 King Street / 153 King Street / Upper Pearson Street / George Street
The **Pineapple** was a corner pub, prominently situated on the north-east corner of King
Street and Upper Pearson Street. *First Record: 1855 / Last Record: 1940*

PINEAPPLE
43 Duke Street *First Record: Unconfirmed / Last Record: Unconfirmed*

PLOUGH
Dotwick Street *First Record: 1834 / Last Record: 1834*

POLKA
11 Bell Street
The Polka is a lively dance which originated in Bohemia, and there is no obvious
connection, or reason why this pub was so named.
First Record: 1865 / Last Record: 1865

PORTER VAT
Ropery Bank / Ropery Walk
Porter is a dark well hopped beer made from brown malt. The name came about as a
result of its popularity with street and river porters, and the connection with a pub is
apparent. *First Record: Unconfirmed / Last Record: Unconfirmed*

PORTHOLE (Refer to: GOLDEN FLEECE)
11 New Quay

POST BOY
42 Stephenson Street
The **Post Boy** stood on the east side of Stephenson Street, and slightly to the north of its
junction with Charlotte Street. The name was probably derived from the nearby post
office, with similar connections to the **Old Post Office Inn** which stood close by on
Tyne Street adjacent to the Post Office Stairs. *First Record: 1850 / Last Record: 1865*

POWBURN
97-98 Bedford Street
The **Powburn** is a new and modern pub to North Shields. The premises which were formerly shops were converted to form a public house during 2007.
First Record: 2007 / Last Record: Extant 2013

PRINCE ALBERT
39 Church Street *First Record: 1869 / Last Record: 1871*

PRINCE ALBERT
Hayhole
The exact location of the **Prince Albert** is unconfirmed, but was believed situated near the River Tyne in the Hayhole Road area.
First Record: Unconfirmed / Last Record: Unconfirmed

PRINCE COBURG
Clive Street / Bird-in-Hand Quay
The name of this pub was derived from Queen Victoria's connection with Prince Albert who descended from the German House of Saxe-Coburg and Gotha.
First Record: 1822 / Last Record: 1834

PRINCE OF PRUSSIA
7 Clive Street
It is likely that this pub was named in honour of Prince Heinrich of Prussia, who was born in 1862 and was the third of eight children born to Crown Prince Friedrich III (later Emperor Friedrich III), and Victoria, Princess Royal of Great Britain, a daughter of the British Queen Victoria. *First Record: 1865 / Last Record: 1865*

PRINCE OF WALES TAVERN
31 Liddell Street / 32 Liddell Street / Bell Street / Custom House Quay
This building is one of the oldest public houses still operating in North Shields, and records indicate that a pub has stood on this site since the early 1600s. The **Prince of Wales** (*above, c. 1896*) was at one time one of the largest taverns in the Low Town, and occupied a site on what was then a very narrow Liddell Street. It was originally nicknamed and referred to as 'The Old Wooden Doll', because of the famous Wooden

Dolly figurehead associated with the North Shields fishing trade, which stood outside the premises in the adjacent alleyway on Custom House Quay.

There have been several Wooden Dollies at this location, the first of which was erected in 1814 by Alexander Bartleman, a local Shipowner and Brewer. It soon became a traditional custom for superstitious sailors to carve off a sliver of wood from the figure, believing it would bring them good luck before they set off on a voyage, as a result of which, it was completely destroyed within a few years, resulting in another one being made and erected in 1820, which eventually suffered the same fate.

In June 1864, a third Wooden Doll was made and set in place beside the pub but in the late 1890s, it was broken in two, prompting calls for yet another replacement.

The fourth Doll was made in 1902, a copy of which was placed in Northumberland Square in 1958.

Following the decline of the fishing industry, the **Prince of Wales** closed for a number of years during the mid 1970s until its acquisition by Sam Smith's Brewery, of Tadcaster, who reopened it in 1992 after carrying out an extensive refurbishment. The brewery arranged for a replacement copy of the third Wooden Doll to be returned to its original site next to the pub. *First Record: 1850 / Last Record: Extant 2013*

PRINCE OF WALES
7-8 Union Street / Causey Bank
The **Prince of Wales** occupied a position to the east of Causey Bank, on the south side of Union Street, opposite the **Golden Lion Inn**.
First Record: 1855 / Last Record: 1940

PRINCE OF WALES FEATHERS
51 Liddell Street
The name of this pub is derived from the heraldic badge, usually associated with the Prince of Wales, which in its modern form symbolises three white feathers encircled by a coronet with the motto; 'Ich Dien'. Situated on Liddell Street, North Shields, this inn was later renamed as the **Princess of Wales**.
First Record: 1855 / Last Record: 1855

PRINCESS OF WALES
(Refer to: **PRINCE OF WALES FEATHERS**)
51 Liddell Street

PRIORY INN
2 Albert Terrace *First Record: Unconfirmed / Last Record: Unconfirmed*

PUB & KITCHEN (Refer to: **QUEENS HEAD**)
Albion Road

The Prince of Wales, Union Street / Causey Bank, c.1930.

PUNCHEON
39 Union Street
The **Puncheon** stood on the north side of Union Street, between Church Way and Bedford Street, and probably took its name from a Puncheon, which is an old word, referring to a cask with a capacity of between 70 and 120 gallons. Prior to 1887, the name was changed to the **Rector House**.
*First Record: 1865 as the **Puncheon** / Last Record: 1899 as the **Rector House***

PUSH AND PULL INN
3 Bedford Street
The unusually named **Push and Pull Inn** was situated almost at the foot of, and on the east side of Bedford Street. It occupied a situation on the steepest part of the road,

backing onto Church Stairs. By 1887, it had been renamed the **Bridge Inn**, probably named after the nearby area called Wooden Bridge.
*First Record: 1850 as the **Push & Pull Inn** / Last Record: 1899 as the **Bridge Inn***

QUAY TAP HOUSE
50 Bell Street
Although not strictly an inn or tavern in the true sense of the meaning, it is one of a new generation of premises best described as a bar café. It is one of the most recent 'pubs' to become established in North Shields which has evolved with the regeneration of the Fish Quay. *First Record: 2010 / Last Record: Extant 2013*

QUEENS HEAD
Turnpike Road / 8 Albion Street / 11 Albion Street / 13 Albion Road / 14 Albion Road

The Queens Head, Albion Road, c.2005.

When Queen Victoria ascended the throne in 1837, her name became quite the rage and was applied to all manner of subjects. The house which stands on the south-east corner of Church Way and Albion Road was originally called the **Kings Head**, before the then landlord, William Weatherilt changed the name to the **Victoria Inn**, and accompanied the name change by fixing a painted portrait of the 'maiden monarch' as the signboard of his inn. For many years afterwards, the inn was affectionately known as the '*Church House*' because of its close relationship with Christ Church which stood opposite. On christening days, it is said that men stood around in readiness to take upon themselves the responsibilities of Godfathers for a shilling, returning to the inn to drink the fee! On marriage occasions, a bride when otherwise unprovided, could be 'given away' on the same easy terms as those required for christenings. Women, after being 'churched', sometimes required a stimulant for nervous exhaustion. After burials in the church yard, a 'sit-down' by the under bearers became a regular thing. Bell-ringing also contributed its quota to the good of the house, for the bell-ringers in those days sometimes drank at the inn from the finish of the Sunday morning peal until their bell tower ascent in the afternoon.

The stagecoaches running between Shields and Newcastle, and between Shields and Blyth, took up and set off passengers here. Coachmen would chat with the landlord or landlady, and there were generally two or three servant girls to assist with the luggage. In later years, the name of the inn changed from the **Victoria Inn** to the **Queens Head**.

Following a general decline in the pub trade, the premises closed in 2012 and underwent refurbishment work to re-open later that year under a new name of the **Pub & Kitchen**. *First Record: 1822 / Last Record: Extant 2013*

QUEENS HEAD

Lower Pearson Street
The **Queens Head** stood on the north side of Lower Pearson Street (later Charlotte Street), at its junction with Queen Street.
First Record: Unconfirmed / Last Record: Unconfirmed

QUEENS HEAD

Ferry Boat Landing *First Record: 1834 / Last Record: 1834*

QUEENS HEAD

Low Lights / Back Union Road
The **Queens Head** was a very small inn, and part of the area known as the Low Lights. It was situated to the east of, and behind Union Road near Cliffords Fort. The neighbouring **Hope and Anchor** stood directly next door to it.
First Record: 1855 / Last Record: 1887

RABY CASTLE

38 Tyne Street *First Record: 1834 / Last Record: 1834*

RAFFLED ANCHOR (Refer to: ANCHOR TAVERN)

Swans' Quay / Clive Street / 14 Duke Street / 18 Duke Street

RAILWAY TAVERN (Refer to: UNCLE TOM'S CABIN)

51 Bedford Street

RAILWAY HOTEL

6 Railway Street / Little Bedford Street
This building was situated on the south side of Railway Street at the north corner with Little Bedford Street. It underwent three name changes during its lifetime.
*First Record: 1850-85 as the **Railway Hotel** / Second Record: 1886-87 as the **Rutherford Hotel** / Last Record: 1897-1930 as the **Station Hotel***

RAILWAY INN

63 Nile Street
As the name suggests the building took its name from North Shields Railway Station which, separated by an alleyway on the west side of Nile Street, stood directly next to it. In 1861, the building was known as the **Railway Inn**, later to become the **Railway Hotel**, (not be confused with another nearby premises of the same name which stood directly opposite on the east side of the road).

The building was one of just a small number in the town which had a glazed terracotta faience, and ornamental signage above the windows and doors, however, after it closed down as a public house during the 1990s, the premises were converted to accommodate an amusement

North Shields Railway Station with the Railway Hotel beyond, Nile Street, c.1912.

arcade. Part of the original brown glazed terracotta faience is still apparent, but modern plastic signage covers the original ornamental pub name.
First Record: 1865 / Last Record: 1990s

RAILWAY TAVERN
57 Clive Street
An unusual name for a tavern in this part of North Shields, as there is no obvious connection with a railway in this area.
First Record: Unconfirmed /
Last Record: Unconfirmed

RECTOR HOUSE (Refer to: PUNCHEON)
39 Union Street

RED LAMP HOTEL
57 Clive Street / Ratcliff's Bank
The Red Lamp Hotel (*right, c.1898*) was situated on the west side of Clive Street, adjacent to the south side of Ratcliffs Bank Stairs. *First Record: 1887 / Last Record: 1930*

The Lindsay Arms, in the foreground, opposite the Red Lamp Hotel.

RED LION INN
Church Road / 37 Church Way / 103 Church Way / 104 Church Way / 105 Church Way / 27 Wellington Street
It is very difficult to imagine that the **Red Lion Inn**, also known as the **Old Red Lion** was at one time a popular roadside inn, which stood in the midst of green fields and hawthorn hedges, at a time when Church Way was nothing more than a narrow road, lined on each side by green hedgerows, and not another house within call. It was probably one of the oldest inns recorded in North Shields, and is shown on a plan of the Manor of Tynemouth dated 1757. The pub was demolished by the then owner, Mr. A.N. Dodds, who later rebuilt the premises on the corner of Church Way and Wellington Street, backing on to Camden Lane.
First Record: 1757 / Last Record: 1940

Left: Red Lion Inn, boarded up after closure, Church Way, c.1968.

REFORM TAVERN
North Street
First Record: 1834 / Last Record: 1850

REGATTA TAVERN
49 Tyne Street
The **Regatta Tavern** was a small pub, which stood at the top of the bank side on the south side of Tyne Street almost opposite the junction with Linskill Street. It was renamed as the **Turf Hotel** sometime prior to 1897.
*First Record: 1850 as the **Regatta Tavern** / Last Record: 1912 as the **Turf Hotel***

RISING SUN
4 Toll Street
Although recorded as a separate public house, it is likely that this is the same building as the **Rising Sun Inn**, situated on the corner of Beacon Street and Tyne Street.
First Record: 1834 / Last Record: 1834

RISING SUN INN

1 Beacon Street / Tyne Street
The **Rising Sun Inn** (*below, c.1930*) was a corner pub, situated on the bank top, at the south-west corner of Beacon Street and Tyne Street, opposite the original High Beacon Lighthouse forming part of Trinity Buildings. *First Record: 1850 / Last Record: c.1957*

RISING SUN INN

Brunswick Place, Coble Dene / Burdon Main, Coble Dene / Albert Edward Dock, Coble Dene
The **Rising Sun Inn** stood on the north side of Brunswick Place, a few yards to the east of the **King William IV Public House**.
First Record: 1834 / Last Record: 1940

ROB ROY

Clive Street
Named after the Scottish clan leader and outlaw whose banditry is the subject of Sir Walter Scott's novel 'Rob Roy' in 1817. *First Record: 1855 / Last Record: 1855*

ROBERT BURNS TAVERN (Refer to: BURNS TAVERN)

Clive Street / Broad Quay

ROBBIE BURNS INN (Refer to: BURNS TAVERN)

Clive Street / Bell Street / Custom House Quay / Broad Quay

ROBIN HOOD

21 Beacon Street / Bird Street
The **Robin Hood** was situated at the eastern end of Charlotte Street, at the north-west corner of Beacon Street and Bird Street. During an air raid in 1941, the building suffered some bomb damage, and was demolished in 1957, to be replaced by the **Corvette** pub.
First Record: 1850 / Last Record: 1957

Left: The Robin Hood Inn, Beacon Street, following a bombing raid in 1941.

ROCKCLIFF ARMS

15 Bedford Street *First Record: 1897 / Last Record: 1897*

ROEBUCK

Liddell Street
A roebuck is a male roe deer, which gave its name to this pub.
First Record: 1822 / Last Record: 1827

ROSE INN

4 Dene Street, Mount Pleasant / New Row, Mount Pleasant

The **Rose Inn** stood on the east side of the road, towards the northern end of Dene Street. *First Record: 1834 / Last Record: 1940*

ROSE AND CROWN
Liddell Street
After the Battle of Bosworth Field in which Richard III was killed, the victor, Henry Tudor proclaimed himself Henry VII. Henry had no real claim to the Throne of England, so had to legitimise his position. This he did by marrying someone who did have a claim: Princess Elizabeth of York. She was so beautiful she was known as the Rose of York, hence the commemorating pub name. The Rose is Princess Elizabeth, and the Crown is Henry VII. *First Record: 1822 / Last Record: 1834*

ROSE AND CROWN
Tyne Street
High on the bank top, and adjoining Turpin's Bank Stairs, the **Rose and Crown** stood opposite the foot of Stephenson Street, at its junction with Tyne Street. *First Record: 1855 / Last Record: 1855*

ROSE OF ALLENDALE
24 Bell Street
This public house was undoubtedly named after a song composed in the 1840s by Charles Jeffries and Sidney Nelson, and entitled 'The Rose of Allendale', the lyrics of which refer to a maiden from the town of Allendale, Northumberland. *First Record: 1865 / Last Record: 1865*

ROYAL ALBERT HOTEL
Dene Terrace / Dene Street / Dock Road
This hotel was probably named in honour of Albert Edward, the Prince of Wales, who officially opened the nearby dock in 1884, which also came to bear his name. It was situated on Dock Road, at the corner of Dene Terrace and Dene Street. *First Record: 1887 / Last Record: 1940*

ROYAL ARMS
49 Nile Street / 59 Nile Street / 60-61 Nile Street
The **Royal Arms** is a Victorian building, situated on the west side of Nile Street at its junction with Russell Street. The pub bears the unofficial nickname; *'Charlie Robson's'* which was derived from an impressionable and well respected manager called Charles Robson, who ran the pub during the war years from 1936 and well into the 1940s. *First Record: 1850 / Last Record: Extant 2013*

ROYAL OAK
61 Bell Street
The **Royal Oak** stood on the south side of Bell Street, opposite the foot of Lighthouse Bank, and backed directly onto the River Tyne at Dawson's Quay.

After the Battle of Worcester 1651 in the English Civil War, the defeated Prince Charles escaped the scene with the Roundheads on his tail. He managed to reach Shifnal in Shropshire, where he found an oak tree (now know as the Boscobel Oak). He climbed the tree and hid in it for a day while the obviously short-sighted Parliamentarians strolled around under the tree looking for him. After the hunters gave up, Prince Charles came down and escaped to France. He became King Charles II on the Restoration of the Monarchy. To celebrate this good fortune, 29th May (Charles' birthday) was declared Royal Oak Day and the pub name commemorates this. *First Record: 1822 / Last Record: 1887*

ROYAL OAK
Steam Mill Lane, Mount Pleasant
The **Royal Oak** was a large public house which stood just off Dotwick Street, at the end of Buckham's Lane near the perimeter of the Mount Pleasant iron foundry. *First Record: 1865 / Last Record: 1867*

ROYAL QUAYS
Coble Dene

The historic Albert Edward Dock was opened in 1884 by Albert Edward, Prince of Wales. The large modern development built around the dock area was called the Royal Quays because of the early Royal connection. Likewise, the nearby **Royal Quays** public house is a modern building which derives its name from this area and is geared towards tourists and families. *First Record: 1996 / Last Record: Extant 2013*

ROYAL STANDARD
Clive Street / Shepherds Quay *First Record: 1822 / Last Record: 1827*

RUTHERFORD HOTEL (Refer to: RAILWAY HOTEL)
6 Railway Street

SADDLE INN
5 Norfolk Street / 7 Norfolk Street

The **Saddle Inn** was situated on the east side of Norfolk Street, not far from the junction with Tyne Street. *First Record: 1850 / Last Record: 1899*

SAILORS RETURN (Refer to: GEORGE IV)
45 Bell Street / 91 Bell Street / Shepherds Quay

SALMON INN
8 North Street / 13 North Street / 22 North Street / Milbourne Place

The **Salmon Inn** stood on the east side of North Street, not far from the junction with Brunswick Place. *First Record: 1822 / Last Record: 1920*

SALUTATION
Bell Street

A salutation is any word or words used as a greeting, and this was typically a popular choice of names for many English public houses. *First Record: 1822 / Last Record: 1822*

SARACENS HEAD
Liddell Street

The **Saracens Head** was at one time a fairly common name for many public houses throughout the country. In older western historical literature, the Saracens were the people of the Saracen Empire, another name for the Arab Caliphate under the rule of the Umayyad and Abbasid dynasties. The Saracens are credited with many mathematical advances and inventions used in the modern world.
First Record: 1834 / Last Record: 1834

SAWYERS ARMS
Bell Street

The **Sawyers Arms** was situated on the north side of Bell Street, adjoining the foot of King George Stairs, and diagonally opposite the **Nags Head**. Sawyer is an old occupational term referring to someone who saws wood.
First Record: 1855 / Last Record: 1855

SAW MILL INN
Northumberland Street

Speculation suggests that this public house was named after a nearby sawmill.
First Record: 1852 / Last Record: 1852

SCOTCH ARMS
Broad Quay *First Record: 1847 / Last Record: 1847*

SEVEN STARS

1 Wooden Bridge

The **Seven Stars** (*right, c.1920*) was located at the area known as Wooden Bridge, which is the road at the foot of Bedford Street where it forms the junction with Liddell Street.

First Record: 1822 / Last Record: 1930

SEVEN STARS

1 Bell Street / 89 Bell Street / 109 Bell Street / Liddell Street / Seven Stars Quay

The **Seven Stars** on Bell Street had exactly the same name as a neighbouring pub, just a few hundred yards away on Wooden Bridge, and confusion between the two must have been commonplace. This pub however, was situated on the south side of the road, directly next door to the **Prince of Wales Tavern**, and adjacent to Seven Stars Quay.

First Record: 1822 / Last Record: 1899

SHADES

Ranters Bank / Howard Street

This unusually named pub occupied the lower floor of the Old Subscription Library and Maritime Chambers, which later became the Stag Line offices. *First Record: 1850 / Last Record: 1865*

SHAKESPEARE

Lishmans Quay

William Shakespeare (1564-1616), the English poet and playwright, had a number of inns named after him throughout the country. *First Record: 1834 / Last Record: 1850*

SHAKESPEARE INN

17 Clive Street / 31 Clive Street / 33 Clive Street / Shepherds Quay

The **Shakespeare Inn**, or the **Old Shakespeare Tavern,** was a corner building, standing almost opposite the **Exchange Inn**, and situated on the east side of Clive Street to the north side of its junction with Shepherds Quay. It stood just a few feet away from the **Victoria Inn**, located on the opposite corner of Shepherds Quay and Clive Street.

First Record: 1822 / Last Record: 1897

SHAKESPEARE TAVERN

Howard Street / 41 Tyne Street / News Room Bank

The **Shakespeare Tavern** was situated on the bank side, at the foot of Howard Street, behind buildings on the south side of Tyne Street with News Room Stairs running alongside and down the bank to Liddell Street. The name was changed in later years to the **Burton House**, which may have been to avoid confusion with the nearby **Shakespeare Inn** on Clive Street.

First Record: 1855 as the **Shakespeare Tavern** *Last Record: 1938 as the* **Burton House**

SHEPHERDESS INN

102 Bell Street / Anchor Quay / Shepherdess Quay

The **Shepherdess Inn** stood on the south side of Bell Street, backing on to the River Tyne and Anchor Quay. *First Record: 1822 / Last Record: 1899*

SHIP INN

Steels Quay *First Record: 1834 / Last Record: 1850*

SHIP
64 Bell Street / 65 Bell Street / 78 Bell Street / 80 Bell Street
The **Ship Inn** stood on the south side of Bell Street, opposite to, and not far from the bottom of the High Lighthouse stairs. The inn backed onto the River Tyne between Mathwins Quay and Dawsons Quay. *First Record: 1822 / Last Record: 1899*

SHIP
Clive Street / Shepherds Quay *First Record: 1822 / Last Record: 1827*

SHIP
Toll Square *First Record: 1822 / Last Record: 1827*

SHIP
22 Bull Ring *First Record: 1834 / Last Record: 1834*

SHIP
24 Middle Street / 55 Middle Street
The **Ship Inn** stood on the west side of Middle Street, diagonally opposite the **Wheatsheaf Inn**. *First Record: 1822 / Last Record: 1938*

SHIP HOPEWELL
Duke Street
This inn may have been named after the explorer, Henry Hudson's first command on the ship, 'The Hopewell', which was an aging, 40-ton barque with a small crew. In 1606, John Knight had already sailed the Hopewell in search of the Northwest Passage along the coast of Labrador. 'The Hopewell' was also a ship which carried immigrants from Great Britain to New England in 1634. *First Record: 1827 / Last Record: 1827*

SHIP TAVERN
14 Clive Street
The **Ship Tavern** stood on the western side of Clive Street, adjacent with Dawsons Bank to the north of the building. *First Record: 1822 / Last Record: 1834*

SHIP AND WHALE
20 Bell Street *First Record: 1822 / Last Record: 1855*

SHIP LADY JANE
Bell Street
The suggestion is that this pub name was derived from a ship or vessel called 'Lady Jane', and probably named after Lady Jane Grey (1537-54), a great-grand-daughter of Henry VII who reigned as uncrowned queen regnant of England for nine days in 1553. *First Record: 1834 / Last Record: 1834*

SHIP IN LAUNCH (Refer to: MASONS ARMS)
Low Lights / Back Union Road / Tanners Bank

SHIPWRIGHTS ARMS
Clive Street / Bell Street *First Record: 1822 / Last Record: 1827*

SHIPWRIGHTS ARMS
Church Way
The **Shipwrights Arms** stood on the west side of Church Way, a little to the south of its junction with Saville Street. *First Record: 1855 / Last Record: 1855*

SHOULDER OF MUTTON
19 Wellington Street *First Record: 1822 / Last Record: 1834*

SHOULDER OF MUTTON
Clive Street / Ferry Boat Landing *First Record: 1822 / Last Record: 1850*

SIR COLIN CAMPBELL
3 Saville Street West

The **Sir Colin Campbell** public house is situated on the north side of Saville Street West, diagonally opposite the **Ballarat Hotel**. During its lifetime, the front of the building was completely altered, almost being rebuilt. The pub was named as a tribute to Field Marshall Sir Colin Campbell (also known as Lord Clyde), who was an outstanding soldier, born in Glasgow in 1792. Campbell fought in the Peninsular Wars (1808-14), the Sikh War (1848-49), The Crimean War (1854), and the Indian Mutiny of 1857. Campbell died in 1863, and is buried in Westminster Abbey. He is remembered for his personal bravery and, as a senior commander, for his cautious and considered prosecution of his various campaigns which saved the lives of many of his men. The **Sir Colin Campbell** closed as a pub in 2011 and became a retail shop.

First Record: 1865 / Last Record: 2011

SIR WILLIAM WALLACE
Clive Street

Named after William Wallace, who was one of Scotland's greatest national heroes, and the undisputed leader of the Scottish resistance forces during the first years of the long and ultimately successful struggle to free Scotland from English rule at the end of the 13th century. He was knighted in December 1297 and proclaimed guardian of the kingdom. *First Record: 1855 / Last Record: 1855*

SPIRIT OF DUBLIN PORTER VAULTS (Refer to: FLINNS and the NORTH EASTERN HOTEL)
Nile Street / West Percy Street

Originally called the **Spirit of Dublin Porter Vaults**, and standing on the corner of Nile Street and West Percy Street, these premises later became better known as **Flinns**. *First Record: Unconfirmed / Second Record: 1847-97 as Flinns / Last Record: 1897-1968 as the North Eastern Hotel.*

SPRING GARDENS INN
(Refer to: **FLOWER POT**)
Albion Street / 14 Albion Road West

Right: Spring Gardens Inn, Albion Road West, c.1890.

Below right: Spring Gardens Inn, Albion Road West, c.1934.

STAITH HOUSE
57 Low Lights / Union Road

Situated opposite the foot of Brewhouse Bank, and to the east of Union Road near Cliffords Fort the **Staith House** stood in the area known as the Low Lights. It was renamed as the **New Dolphin** prior to 1865. The inn is typically a fisherman's pub which has been modernised and extended over the years. *First Record: 1850 as the **Staith House** / Last Record: Extant 2013 as the **New Dolphin***

STAITH HOUSE
Whitehill Point *First Record: 1847 / Last Record: 1847*

STANLEY ARMS
70 Rudyerd Street / 1-2 Stanley Street
Occupying a site on the corner of
Stanley Street and Rudyerd Street, it has
long been thought that the **Stanley
Arms** was named after the steamship
'SS Stanley', which ran aground on the
Black Middens, in 1864. This is not the
case as the pub itself actually pre-dates
the shipwreck. The likelihood is that it
derived its name from the street on
which it stands, ie; Stanley Street,
named after Edward (Lord) Stanley
who was Prime Minister three times
between 1852 and 1868. The pub had a
stained glass fanlight window depicting

A stained glass window depicting the Stanley Arms, Rudyerd Street / Stanley Street.

a paddle steamer which was thought to be a representation of the 'SS Stanley', however
this is inaccurate because the 'SS Stanley' was in fact a propeller-driven vessel. The
premises have seen several alterations and modernisations during its existence and
after acquiring a poor reputation since the 1990s, an effort was made in 2012 to clear
the tarnished image which included a name change to the **Fleet**.
*First Record: 1863 as the **Stanley Arms** / Last Record: Extant 2013 as the **Fleet***

STAR
19 Camden Street *First Record: 1834 / Last Record: 1834*

STAR
1 Wellington Street / 2 Wellington Street / 4 Wellington Street
The **Star Inn** was a small building occupying a site on the north side of Wellington
Street, near the corner with Little Bedford Street. *First Record: 1850 / Last Record: 1887*

*Left: The Star Inn
Wellington Street, c.1886.*

STAR INN (Refer to: STAR AND GARTER)
26/28 Clive Street / Star
and Garter Quay

STAR AND GARTER
26/28 Clive Street / Star
and Garter Quay
The **Star and Garter** (also
known as the **Star Inn**),
was one of the larger Low
Town inns, which was
situated on the east side
of Clive Street, opposite
the foot of Wascoes Bank
Stairs and stood next
door to the **Lindsay
Arms**. The pub is
believed to date back as
far as the Tudor period
and existed into the
1920s. The length of the
building ran adjacent to

the Star and Garter Quay with the rear edge of the building overlooking the River Tyne.

The name 'Star and Garter' originates from the insignia belonging to the Order of the Garter founded by King Edward III in 1344. The Order of the Garter is the oldest and most prestigious order of chivalry in the United Kingdom.
First Record: 1822 / Last Record: 1899

Right: The Star and Garter, Clive Street, c.1886.

STARLING
24 South Street / East Street / Milburn Place
The **Starling Inn** was a corner building, which stood on the north-east apex of East Street, as it curved south into South Street, Mount Pleasant.
First Record: 1850 / Last Record: 1899

STATION HOTEL (Refer to: RAILWAY HOTEL)
6 Railway Street

STEAM BOAT (Refer to: FERRY HOUSE)
1 Duke Street

STEAM FERRY HOUSE (Refer to: FERRY HOUSE)
1 Duke Street / New Quay

STEAM MILL INN
Mount Pleasant *First Record: 1855 / Last Record: 1855*

STEAM MILL INN
Clive Street / Black Lion Quay / Steam Mill Lane *First Record: 1822 / Last Record: 1834*

STEAM PACKET (Refer to FERRY HOUSE)
1 Duke Street / New Quay

STONE HOUSE INN
12 Clive Street / Black Cock Quay
The **Stone House Inn** was situated on the east side of Clive Street, almost opposite the foot of Linskills Bank Stairs, between Black Cock Quay and the Jerusalem Coffee House Quay. *First Record: 1855 / Last Record: 1899*

SUN
Stephenson Street *First Record: 1822 / Last Record: 1827*

SUN INN (Refer to: ADMIRAL JERVIS)
73 Bell Street

SUN INN
7 North Street / 13 North Street *First Record: 1847 / Last Record: 1847*

SUNDERLAND BRIDGE

9 Clive Street

The old Sunderland Bridge which once carried the Great North Road across the River Wear consisted of four semicircular stone arches and dates back to the 14th century, but why such a name was chosen for a North Shields pub is uncertain.

The **Sunderland Bridge** was a small inn, located on the east side of Clive Street and backing on to Black Cock Quay. It occupied a site on the south corner of the narrow passageway leading to Scarp Landing. *First Record: 1822 / Last Record: 1887*

SUSPENSION BRIDGE

Clive Street / 4 Bedford Street

Plans for a suspension bridge across the River Tyne to link North and South Shields were drawn up in 1824. Although this pub originated two years earlier, it is possible that the initial proposals may have had some bearing on the name.
First Record: 1822 / Last Record: 1834

SUSSEX ARMS

6 Duke Street / 34 Duke Street

Situated directly opposite the **Phoenix Inn**, the **Sussex Arms** stood on the east side of Duke Street. A narrow alleyway separated it from the tiny **Steam Boat Public House** which stood next door. *First Record: 1850 / Last Record: 1865*

SWAN

Clive Street *First Record: 1822 / Last Record: 1822*

SWEDISH ARMS

Bell Street

The origins of this public house name probably relate to the vast numbers of Swedish seamen who visited North Shields from the mid 1800s.
First Record: 1855 / Last Record: 1855

TAP AND SPILE (Refer to: VICTORIA HOTEL)

1 Albert Terrace / Tynemouth Road

TEAC FIDDLERS (Refer to: ALNWICK CASTLE)

Saville Street

TELEGRAPH HOTEL / TELEGRAPH INN

3 Nile Street

The tiny pub known as the **Telegraph** was located on the east side of Nile Street, directly opposite North Shields Railway Station. 1861 ordnance survey maps indicate that it was originally called the **Railway Hotel**, but by 1896, had been renamed as the **Telegraph Hotel**, probably to avoid confusion with the similarly named and larger **Railway Inn / Railway Hotel** which stood on the opposite side of the road. After closure as a public house, the **Telegraph** was converted to become a shop.
First Record: 1865 / Last Record: 1968

TERRACE INN

1 East Stephenson Street / 1 Dale Terrace / Tynemouth Road

The **Terrace Inn** stood almost directly opposite the Brandling Terrace Memorial Church. The inn actually stood on the corner of East Stephenson Street at its junction with Tynemouth Road. East Stephenson Street has long since been demolished and redeveloped, and was replaced with the Magistrates Court and part of North Shields Police Station. *First Record: 1855 / Last Record: 1940*

THREE BULLS HEADS

2 Albion Road *First Record: 1938 / Last Record: 1938*

THREE BULLS HEADS
Union Road / Union Street / Low Lights
The name of this pub is probably derived from English Heraldry, where the insignia depicting three bulls heads was first initiated by Sir Leonard de Sanderstead c.1200. *First Record: 1822 / Last Record: 1834*

THREE MARINERS
Duke Street *First Record: 1822 / Last Record: 1827*

THREE TUNS
4 Wooden Bridge
Near to the bottom of Bedford Street, just south of the Tiger Stairs and directly opposite the foot of Church Stairs, the **Three Tuns** was the neighbouring pub to the **Tiger Inn**. A tun, a large cask for liquids, especially wine, or a mash tun, is an insulated vessel with a false bottom used in brewing. The three tuns are based on the arms of both the Worshipful Company of Vinters and the Worshipful Company of Brewers (City of London Guilds). *First Record: 1822 / Last Record: 1865*

TIGER INN
123 Bedford Street
A well known landmark, the Tiger Stairs are one of the most famous sets of bank stairs in North Shields, and the **Tiger Inn** occupied a position immediately next to and on the south side of these steps. Whether the **Tiger Inn** was named after the stairs, or whether the Tiger Stairs were named after the inn is open to debate!
First Record: 1855 / Last Record: 1928

The Tiger Inn, Bedford Street, c.1928.

TOP HOUSE (Refer to: ALBION INN)
30 Nile Street / 17 Albion Road

TRAVELLERS REST
9 Liddell Street *First Record: 1865 / Last Record: 1865*

TRAWLERS ARMS
Liddell Street

The **Trawlers Arms** was a small pub, situated on the south side of Liddell Street. It stood directly next door to the **Dock Hotel**, and directly opposite the much larger **Black Bull Inn**. The name had an obvious connection with the then busy fishing port of North Shields. *First Record: Unconfirmed / Last Record: Unconfirmed*

TURF HOTEL (Refer to: REGATTA TAVERN)
49 Tyne Street / Church Row

TURF HOTEL
Church Row

A directory listing, dated 1827, exists for the **Turf Hotel**, Church Row, however there is evidence from other directories that the name of the **Turf Hotel** only came into being sometime between 1850 and 1897, when the **Regatta Tavern** on Church Row changed its name. It is therefore likely that there were two premises in close proximity by the name of the **Turf Hotel**. *First Record: 1827 / Last Record: 1827*

TURKS HEAD
6 Linskill Street / 10 Linskill Street

The **Turks Head** stood on the east side of Linskill Street, just a few yards north of the junction with Tyne Street. *First Record: 1850 / Last Record: 1938*

TURKS HEAD
33 Duke Street

The **Turks Head** stood on the west side of Duke Street, a little to the south of the **Crane House Vaults** and the **Phoenix Inn**. *First Record: 1822 / Last Record: 1930*

TURNPIKE GATE
Linskill Street

A turnpike is a road paid for partly or wholly by fees collected from travellers at tollgates. It derives its name from the hinged bar that prevented passage through such a gate until the toll was paid. The pub possibly derived its name from one of the nearby turnpike roads. *First Record: 1834 / Last Record: 1834*

TYNE HOTEL
19 Clive Street / Bird-in-Hand Quay

The **Tyne Hotel** was situated on the east side of Clive Street, almost opposite the foot of Coulsons Bank Stairs, and adjacent to the Bird-in-Hand Quay.
First Record: 1887 / Last Record: 1899

TYNE INN
42 Camden Street / 43 Camden Street

This inn was situated on Camden Street at the corner of Wellington Street and the area is now enclosed by the North Shields Shopping Mall.
First Record: 1822 / Last Record: 1850

TYNE INN
Tennyson Terrace

This was a small detached building, standing on Tennyson Terrace.
First Record: 1938 / Last Record: 1938

TYNEMOUTH CASTLE
Collingwood Street *First Record: 1822 / Last Record: 1827*

TYNEMOUTH CASTLE TAVERN
19 Church Street / 42 Church Street

The **Tynemouth Castle Tavern** was situated on the east side of Church Street, just a

little to the south of the junction with Lower Pearson Street (Charlotte Street).
First Record: 1850 / Last Record: 1865

UNCLE TOM'S CABIN
25 Bedford Street / 26 Bedford Street / 51 Bedford Street
Uncle Tom's Cabin, also known as **Uncle Tom's Vaults**, was certainly one of the most famous public houses that ever existed in North Shields and perhaps fondly remembered. Originally called the **Railway Tavern**, it was renamed as **Uncle Tom's Cabin** around 1855 after the success of the 1852 novel by the same name, written by Harriet Beecher Stowe.

Towards much of the pub's latter day life, it gained a reputation for having a particularly rowdy and boisterous atmosphere. Uncle Tom's was a very basic pub which was renowned for a higher than average number of brawls which took place there. Fortunately, most of these skirmishes were usually dealt with 'in-house' and often without the need for any police intervention. The pub was an experience to visit but certainly not a place for the feint-hearted to consider having anything less than a quiet drink in. The building stood on the east side of Bedford Street, not far from the junction with Saville Street, and was demolished during the late 1960s and 1970s development phase, to be eventually replaced by part of the North Shields Shopping Mall.
*First Record: 1850-1855 as the **Railway Tavern** /*
*Last Record: 1855-1968 as **Uncle Tom's Cabin***

Uncle Tom's Cabin, Bedford Street, c.1895.

UNCLE TOM'S VAULTS (Refer to: UNCLE TOM'S CABIN)
25 Bedford Street / 26 Bedford Street / 51 Bedford Street

UNION HOTEL (Refer to UNION TAVERN)
37 Liddell Street / Dock Quay

UNION INN (Refer to UNION TAVERN)
37 Liddell Street / Dock Quay

UNION TAVERN
37 Liddell Street / Dock Quay
One of the larger Low Town taverns, the **Union Tavern** was also known as the **Union Inn** or the **Union Hotel**, and stood directly opposite the foot of the Library Stairs, adjacent to Dock Quay, on the south side of Liddell Street.
First Record: 1822 / Last Record: 1899

VICTORIA HOTEL
1 Albert Terrace / Tynemouth Road
Another victim of a time when pub companies found it fashionable to change the name of a long established business; the **Victoria**, on Tynemouth Road, was altered in 1989 to become known as the **Tap and Spile**. This name remained with the premises for a number of years before reverting back to its original name of the **Victoria**. *First Record: 1932 / Last Record: Extant 2013*

Above: The Victoria Hotel, Albert Terrace / Tynemouth Road, c.1933, as a small corner pub.

Left: The Victoria Hotel, c.2000, during the time it had been renamed as The Tap and Spile. The extensions and alterations to the premises are quite evident.

VICTORIA HOTEL (Refer to: YE OLDE HUNDRED)
Albion Road *First Record: 1855-c1897 as the Victoria Hotel*

VICTORIA INN (Refer to: QUEENS HEAD)
Turnpike Road / 8 Albion Street / 11 Albion Street / 13 Albion Road / 14 Albion Road

VICTORIA INN
32 Clive Street / 34 Clive Street / Shepherds' Quay
The **Victoria Inn** was a corner building, standing directly opposite the **Exchange Inn**, and situated on the east side of Clive Street to the south side of its junction with Shepherds Quay. It stood just a few feet away from the **Shakespeare Inn**, located on the opposite corner of Shepherds Quay and Clive Street.
First Record: 1850 / Last Record: 1899

VICTORIA HOTEL (Refer to: VICTORIA INN)
Borough Road / 19 William Street

VICTORIA INN
Borough Road / 19 William Street
Also known as the **Victoria Hotel**, and occupying a corner site at the western end of William Street at its junction with Borough Road, the **Victoria** eventually ceased trading as a public house and closed in 2012. *First Record: 1865 / Last Record: 2012*

The Victoria Inn, Borough Road / William Street, c.1960.

VICTORY
Duke Street *First Record: 1834 / Last Record: 1834*

VOLUNTEER ARMS
37 Church Way
This public house bears the same address as that of the **Red Lion Inn**. The **Volunteer Arms** stood on the west side of Church Way, a little to the north of its junction with Wellington Street. The site is now occupied by part of the North Shields Shopping Mall. *First Record: 1887 / Last Record: 1930*

VULCAN'S ARMS
24 Dotwick Street
The **Vulcans Arms** stood directly next door to the **Hylton Castle** public house on the west side of Dotwick Street. An Ordnance Survey map dated 1886 indicates that these buildings were superseded by the **Clarendon Hotel**. *First Record: 1850 / Last Record: 1855*

VULCAN TAVERN
Union Road
At a time when this pub was established, it was probably named after Vulcan, the blacksmith God of fire and volcanoes in Roman mythology. *First Record: 1834 / Last Record: 1834*

WAGON INN
1 Low Lights / Union Road
The **Wagon Inn** was one of a number of buildings forming the area around the Low Lights. It was situated on the east side of Union Road near to Cliffords Fort. The neighbouring **Half Moon Inn** stood behind it, and slightly offset from the rear of this building. *First Record: 1850 / Last Record: 1930*

WAGON INN
Dotwick Street, Mount Pleasant / Milburn Place, Mount Pleasant / 2 New Row, Mount Pleasant
The **Wagon Inn**, originally spelled as 'The Waggon', was situated on the north side of a

short section of street between the end of Burdon Main Row and Dotwick Street, a little to the east of the **Woolsington House Hotel**. The area here was referred to as Mount Pleasant. *First Record: 1822 / Last Record: 1912*

WATERLOO INN
16 Clive Street / 31 Clive Street / 51 Clive Street
Situated between Britannia Bank and Ratcliffs Bank Stairs, slightly to the north of the **Newcastle Arms**, the **Waterloo Inn** occupied a position on the west side of Clive Street, opposite the **Victoria Inn**, and Shepherds Quay. Prior to 1887, the pub was renamed the **Exchange Inn**, or **Exchange Vaults**, and later as the **Exchange Hotel**.
First Record: 1850-87 as the Waterloo Inn /
Last Record: 1887-1938 as the Exchange Inn/Hotel

WATERLOO INN
54 Bedford Street / 103 Bedford Street / 109 Bedford Street
Situated on the east side of Bedford Street, opposite the **Newcastle Inn**, the **Waterloo Inn**, or **Waterloo Tavern** as it was sometimes known, stood slightly to the south of the junction with West Percy Street. *First Record: 1834 / Last Record: 1865*

WELLINGTON HOTEL
Church Way / 5 Wellington Street / 8 Wellington Street / 9 Wellington Street
Recorded as the **Corporation Arms** in 1855, the **Wellington Hotel**, or **Wellington House** stood on the north-west corner of Wellington Street and Church Way.
First Record: 1834 / Last Record: 1940

WELLINGTON HOUSE (Refer to: WELLINGTON HOTEL)
Church Way / 5 Wellington Street / 8 Wellington Street / 9 Wellington Street

WELLINGTON VAULTS
15 Bull Ring / 17 Bull Ring
The **Wellington Vaults** (*below, c.1900*) stood prominently on the western curve of the Bull Ring, almost opposite the northern end of Dotwick Street.
First Record: 1865 / Last Record: 1940

WHEATSHEAF

Limekiln Shore *First Record: 1822 / Last Record: 1834*

WHEATSHEAF

5/7 Collingwood Street
The **Wheatsheaf** was one of the larger public houses in the Bull Ring area, and stood close to the **Wellington Vaults**, on the north side of Collingwood Street, adjacent to the Black Bull Stairs. *First Record: 1834 / Last Record: 1940*

WHEATSHEAF

20 Middle Street / 21 Middle Street
The **Wheatsheaf** stood on the east side of Middle Street, diagonally opposite the **Ship Inn**. *First Record: 1855 / Last Record: 1912*

WHEATSHEAF

6 Liddell Street *First Record: 1822 / Last Record: 1834*

WHITBY ARMS

49 Clive Street *First Record: 1887 / Last Record: 1887*

WHITE HART

49 Bedford Street / 95 Bedford Street
The **White Hart** occupied a site on the east side of Bedford Street, mid way between the junctions with West Percy Street and Wellington Street. A narrow lane next to the pub connected Bedford Street with Church Way.

A 'Hart' is an old word for a stag which was the personal badge of Richard II, who derived it from the arms of his mother, Joan 'The Fair Maid of Kent', heiress of Edmund of Woodstock. The National Gallery, London has a portrait of Richard II wearing a gold and enamelled white hart jewel. Pictures of the angels surrounding the Virgin Mary are often depicted wearing white hart badges, and in English Folklore, the White Hart is associated with Herne the Hunter. There are still many inns and pubs in England that show the sign of the **White Hart**.

By 1993, the pub had developed a somewhat tarnished image, and in an effort to

The White Hart, Bedford Street, c.1964.

overcome this, it was renamed as the **Cask & Stillage**. The name change however was short-lived and in 2001 the pub closed its doors for the last time. Although the building still exists, it was subsequently converted into shops.
First Record: 1850 / Last Record: 2001

WHITE SWAN

Upper Pearson Street
The **White Swan** was a small inn, which stood on the south side of Upper Pearson Street, close to the corner of Linskill Street, and directly opposite to where the present Police Station now stands. *First Record: Unconfirmed / Last Record: Unconfirmed*

WHITE SWAN

Liddell Street *First Record: 1822 / Last Record: 1834*

WILLIAM IV

28 Hudson Street *First Record: Unconfirmed / Last Record: Unconfirmed*

WILLIAM IV

29 Stephenson Street *First Record: 1834 / Last Record: 1834*

WINDSOR CASTLE

Linskill Street *First Record: 1834 / Last Record: 1834*

WOLSINGTON HOUSE HOTEL

Burdon Main Row, Mount Pleasant
The huge **Wolsington House Hotel** (*below, plan from c.1901*) has existed since at least 1834, and was prominently situated on Burdon Main Row, at the corner with Appleby Street. From the mid 1800s, this area was heavily industrialised, particularly as heavy engineering and ship repairing began to gain momentum.

In 1902, the original building was demolished, and rebuilt on exactly the same site, especially to cater for the expanding commerce in this area of North Shields. A stone plaque showing this date was built into a central roof dormer. The 1902 structure is a large imposing two storey red brick building, and originally consisted of a public bar, buffet, dining room, and a smoke room, and was the local call for much of the heavy workforce in the area.
*First Record: 1834 /
Last Record: 2007*

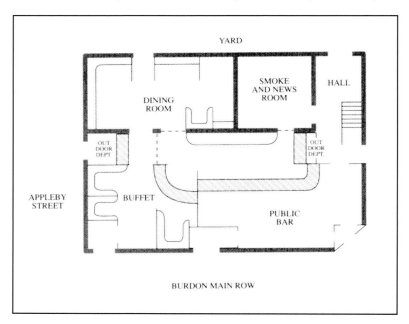

WOODEN BRIDGE HOUSE

Bedford Street
Although unconfirmed, this may actually be the same pub as the **Bridge Inn (Push & Pull)**, situated at No.3 Bedford Street. *First Record: 1865 / Last Record: 1865*

WOODEN DOLL (Refer to: KINGS HEAD)

103 Hudson Street

YARMOUTH ARMS

65 Bell Street *First Record: 1850 / Last Record: 1850*

YARMOUTH ARMS

Duke Street *First Record: 1822 / Last Record: 1822*

The Wooden Doll (formerly the Kings Head), Hudson Street, c.2009.

YE OLDE BORO' ARMS (Refer to: BOROUGH ARMS)
29 Camden Street / 61 Camden Street

YE OLD HUNDRED (Refer to: ANGEL HOTEL & VICTORIA HOTEL)
15 Albion Road / 69 Church Way / 100 Albion Road

Originally called the **Victoria Hotel**, this building was situated next door to the **Angel Hotel** on the south-west corner of Albion Road and Church Way. Just prior to 1897, the **Victoria Hotel** and the **Angel Hotel** were converted to form a single larger building, which became better known as **Ye Olde Hundred**.

Early directories list the addresses as 69 Church Way and sometimes as 15 Albion Road, however after many of the properties were renumbered during the late 1800s; the address of the pub became number 100 Church Way, from which the name of the pub was derived. Refurbishment work in 2012 also saw a slight name change from **Ye Olde Hundred** to simply the **100**.

*First Record: 1855-c1897 as the **Victoria Hotel** / Last Record: Extant 2013 as the **100**.*

Right: Ye Olde Hundred, Albion Road / Church Way, c.1956.

And finally ... THE CABBAGE PATCH

The 'Cabbage Patch' was not a pub, inn or tavern, however it is worthy of a mention in this book because it was perhaps the most well known 'unofficial pub' in North Shields', particularly amongst the fishing community. The 'Cabbage Patch' was situated inside the building known as William Wight's Grocery Store (formerly the Highlander Hotel). Situated on the Union Quay at North Shields, Wight's store once hosted a room which was known to many of the locals as the 'Cabbage Patch'.

The 'Cabbage Patch' was nothing more than a basic vegetable storeroom situated inside the grocery store and was used as a drinking den by many fishermen outside the legal licensing hours of the local pubs. The story of the Cabbage Patch goes back many years, to the days when the fishing industry at North Shields was thriving. Trawlers would berth up on the quay to land their catch with as many as 30 or 40 men working throughout the night.

When the fishermen had completed their overnight work, it was the early hours of the morning, and because none of the local pubs were open at this time, there was nowhere for them to have a well deserved drink.

Wight's Grocery Store however was situated close by and usually opened from 6am which presented many of the fishermen with a golden opportunity. Wight's was originally established as a shipping grocer who supplied a multitude of food provisions to stock the kitchens of the many fishing vessels that berthed at North

Shields Fish Quay. This of course included bottled and canned beers, so it soon became common practice for the fishermen to purchase beer, and consume it in the large internal storeroom of the shop which became popularly known as the 'Cabbage Patch'.

Of course this devious and illicit activity would have never met with, or had the approval of licensing regulations, and so many a blind eye was turned over the years. Bottles of Brown Ale, cans of Export and similar beers were purchased there, however the only practical seating available was on top of the crates and boxes of foodstuffs or sacks of vegetables etc.

Although the seating arrangements failed to deliver the traditional comforts of a local pub, this was matterless to those fishermen who were quite happy to sit around for hours on end in the Cabbage Patch to enjoy their beer and friendly banter before leaving for home or venturing out again for more drink at the local pubs when they opened for business at 10am.

The other benefit of the Cabbage Patch, was that the skippers and shipping agents never had to look very far to re-instate their respective crews.

Quite often it was a simple matter of just popping into the Cabbage Patch and calling 'Last Orders' when it was time for them to return to their vessel in readiness to once again set off to sea for the next fishing trip.

WILLIAM WIGHT LTD

William Wight first established his grocery business at North Shields in December 1926.

The shop premises however started life as the Highlander Hotel around 1834, and after its closure as a public house, the premises were taken over by Wight who opened for trade here in 1929.

The shop provided fishing fleets with bulk stores and provisions.

Over the many years that Wight's grocery business has been established, times have changed dramatically as the fishing industry has all but vanished from North Shields.

At one time, Wight's business was 95% boats and 5% over the counter trade, but now it is a complete reversal with 95% over the counter trade and 5% boats. This in itself is a massive turnaround in the type of customer trade.

Wight's still exist to this day and is still run as a family concern by Marty Ponton, however the business has had to adapt and change to survive. The store has changed from what was primarily a ship supplier to a multipurpose shop which now sell everything from a tin of polish to a pound of best butter or a morning paper to a cup of hot coffee and a bacon sandwich.

Wight's now deal with the general public, regular customers, visitors, tourism and boats at the same time.

The thousands of workers that were once the lifeblood of North Shields Fish Quay have now gone, and have been replaced by thousands of visitors, many of whom come from all over the world to visit the Fish Quay, which includes the humour, hospitality and personal service offered by the staff of Wight's – a very traditional and old fashioned grocery store that somehow manage to retain a very typical old world charm and character.

The shop still opens around 6am, but sadly, the days of the 'Cabbage Patch' have long since gone so it is no longer possible to call in for an early morning beer, however if you're still feeling thirsty, just stop off and buy a few cans or bottles to take home instead!

Marty Ponton behind the counter of Wight's Grocers.

ACKNOWLEGEMENTS

It is only with the assistance and encouragement of others that compilation of this book has been possible. I am therefore particularly grateful to the undermentioned individuals and organisations who have made a contribution in one way or another:

Tyne & Wear Archives, Blenheim Street, Newcastle-upon-Tyne
Staff of North Tyneside Local Studies Library
Alan R. Newton
Geoff Gibson, West Monkseaton
Betty Steel, West Monkseaton
Colin Wilkinson, Preston Village, North Shields
Lillian & Arthur Reeve, (Formerly of 'The Porthole'), North Shields
Marty Ponton, William Wights, North Shields
George Nairn & Andrew Clark

SOURCES OF REFERENCE

DIRECTORIES

Blairs County of Northumberland Directories 1968
Bulmers Directory 1887
Kellys Directories 1894-1938
Parson & Whites Directories 1827-28
Pigots Directories 1822-34
Wards Directories 1850-1940
Whellans Directory 1855

BOOKS

A History of the Pubs & Inns of North Tyneside by Kevin Bradley
English Inns by Thomas Burke
Licensed Premises – Law and Practice by Philip Kolvin
North Shields and Tynemouth by Richard Simpson
The Dictionary of Pub Names by David Rothwell
The Local: A History of the English Pub by Paul Jennings
The Northumbrian Pub by Lynn F. Pearson

MISCELLANEOUS

Northumberland Census Records
Northumbria Police – Licensing Registers
Ordnance Survey Maps
Wikipedia (Internet Based)

Also available from Summerhill Books

North Shields – Stepping Back In Time

Offbeat – Memories of Tynemouth Borough Police

Wallsend Pubs & Clubs

Monkseaton Village Volume One & Two

Crime and Punishment in the North East

Wartime Memories – Stories of the Second World War in the North East

visit our website to view our full range of books:

www.summerhillbooks.co.uk